Praise for Dave Carberry

"Many entrepreneurs worry that asking for help is a sign of weakness, but Dave Carberry shows how Needworking can be a strategy for empowerment."

Seth Goldman
Founder of Honest Tea, Eat the Change and Just Ice Tea

"*Stop Networking Start Needworking* is an in-depth look at the value of weaving your personal values, business strategy, and practical implementation together. Dave Carberry draws from extensive research and decades of networking experience to outline an insightful framework centered around understanding and fulfilling shared Needs.

Committed to building a better model, Needworking adds more significant meaning to our interactions and relationships. For anyone seeking to move beyond superficial networking and establish authentic relationships, Stop Networking Start Needworking is an indispensable guide.

Human interaction and serving the greater good are more important than ever, and Dave provides a framework and platform that serves that purpose!"

Colleen McKenna
LinkedIn Trainer, Strategist, and Advisor
Author, *It's Business, Not Social™*
CEO and Founder, Intero Advisory

A must read for every new or seasoned C-suite executive, containing powerful tools and soul-searching reminders to better position yourself and your business in a post-COVID world. Carberry synthesizes the concepts of leadership, collaboration & making more meaningful connections, as well as the importance of "personal branding" and giving back-- essential for leadership and success at any level, in business and at home.

Lisa Rusyniak
President and CEO, Goodwill Industries of the Chesapeake, Inc.

"*Stop Networking, Start Needworking* is a manual for success.

Far too many people write business books using only half-formed personal philosophies and a few years of experience. Typically, they prove the old adage: those who can't, teach. Dave Carberry is an exception to the proverb.

Not only does he bring years of business experience to the book, but Dave also quotes and cites experts from a broad range of disciplines. His use of references throughout the book lends authority to the Needworking lessons he teaches.

In today's environment of overcrowded mixers, rapid impersonal communications, and congested social media channels, the book gives you specific tools to rise above the pandemonium. *Stop Networking, Start Needworking* is a manual for success."

J. Clifton Slater
Publisher and author of historical fiction books in the *Clay Warrior Stories* series and *A Legion Archer* series.

"In the course of more than a decade of participating in and facilitating business leadership groups, I've been struck by how many professionals fear or dislike networking. Dave shines a light on the path to a better way than randomly slinging business cards. Needworking is thoughtful, useful and impactful. It will make a difference in your professional life."

Jim Rafferty
Author, *Leader by Accident: Lessons in Leadership, Loss and Life*

"Stop Networking, Start Needworking is a must read for any professional desiring to advance and create a successful support system. Dave Carberry is able to break down the complex into simple to understand and common sense approaches to navigating to success. Specifically, The Climb is applicable to everyday life as well as business and echoes my own sentiments and approaches. After serving 32 years on a wrongful conviction and reentering society at age 50, I can personally relate as I embraced this philosophy during my own journey to success."

John N. Huffington
Motivational Speaker and Author of *Innocent: An Obscene Miscarriage of Justice*

"What I love about Needworking is its emphasis on purpose-driven networking. This book isn't just about making connections; it's about making the right connections that matter to you. As someone who's always believed in the power of technology to connect people, 'Needworking' offers a fresh perspective. It's about using your network strategically to meet specific needs, a crucial skill in both business and personal growth.

We all need to recalibrate because social media has given us vast connections that are pretty widespread and lack depth. Needworking guides us back to the essence of meaningful interactions. It's not just who you know; it's about who understands your journey, your needs, your vision. Needworking is networking reimagined for the modern world and this book brilliantly shows us how to forge deeper, more purposeful connections."

Mario Armstrong
NBC Contributor, 2x EMMY Award Winner & Entrepreneur

STOP
Networking
START
Needworking

STOP
Networking
ST△RT
Needworking

The Intersection of
Maslow's Needs and **Networking**

Dave Carberry

Printed in the United States of America.
First edition 2024.

Cover and layout design by G Sharp Design, LLC.
www.gsharpmajor.com

ISBN 979-8-9895244-0-2 (paperback)
ISBN 979-8-9895244-1-9 (ebook)

To my father, James William Carberry,

You were a true fighter, a guiding mentor, my hero, and an extraordinary giver. Your remarkable stories, infectious laughter, and unwavering perseverance in the face of physical adversity have been a constant source of inspiration. This book, *Stop Networking, Start Needworking*, is dedicated to you and to people like you who, through their kindness and support, help others along their journey towards achieving their own version of Maslow's Hierarchy of Needs.

With profound admiration and love,

Dave

TABLE OF CONTENTS

FOREWORD

I had a boss look at me early in my career and he stated, simply, that business is all about relationships. My first reaction was to wonder why I had spent all those years studying engineering and business if the key to success was simply relationships. Thirty-five years later, I find myself making that same statement to the younger folks in our business regularly. It is such a simple concept but riddled with so much complexity.

Social media has only added to the complexity. Concepts such as number of "likes" or number of "followers" have crept into our conversations. How many times have you hit "accept all" on your LinkedIn profile, and then twenty minutes later you can't remember half of the invitations you accepted.

Dave's Needworking concept tackles what many of us feel is missing on other platforms: the human element. Don't collect "likes" and "followers" like baseball cards. Think about each relationship. How can you help each other achieve your individual goals. Build relationships, think about how you can give within the relationship and don't be afraid to ask for things that you need.

We can all use help navigating our goals and dreams. A safe environment established with an underlying theme of helping and giving just makes sense. Many of us struggle to put ourselves out there and ask for help. I playfully call it a case of the "I got its" when someone tells me they've got it and won't accept help when it is obvious that a little help would be, well, helpful.

I appreciate the candor and openness of the book. Dave is not afraid to share the highlights and the lowlights of his own journey which gives the writing a very real, personal feel.

He also effectively pulls in concepts from well-known leadership books to reference and tie together his underlying concepts. He's not trying to reinvent the wheel but rather enhance the way we look at networking today and add more depth and meaning to our relationships.

I read the manuscript front to back in a sitting yesterday. I found it thought provoking, logical and very engaging. I am not a person who naturally or gracefully networks, partially because of the perceived superficiality that comes with the territory. I'm confident Dave's approach will help me work through some of my paradigms as I look at my network of relationships in a fresh light.

Jamie Mann
President
PRS Guitars

INTRODUCTION

I am on a journey, just like each and every one of us, no matter what that journey is. As with every journey, you Need a road map—unless you like to wander. Needworking for me is my process on my journey. It's a process of networking from a person who is a big-idea creative type and horrible at micro tasks and details. I'm happy to share what I believe are the simple key ways for you to improve your own networking and how you build professional relationships. I recently spoke at an event in Tampa, and the clarity of what Needworking is smacked me in my face. It's entering a room full of complete strangers and finding the people who can help you on your own journey. We rely on our circle of people, our network, that we've grown over the years. What if that network isn't working, or what if you just moved to a new region of the world? How do you connect or even reconnect? I'm glad you've taken interest in my journey, and I hope that some of what I've learned along the way will help you on yours.

For me, it's been a long journey. Who in their right mind launches a startup at fifty years old? The concept and name of Needworking came to me as I sat in a Goldman Sachs 10,000 Small Businesses cohort in Baltimore, Maryland. Goldman Sachs 10,000 Small Businesses provides business education, support services, and pathways to capital for growth-oriented entrepreneurs. Participants gain practical skill, to take their business to the next level, covering topics like financial statements, negotiations, and marketing. Participants develop an actionable growth plan for their business with the help of advisors and a network of like-minded entrepreneurs. The program is free for participants and delivered in partnership with academic institutions across the country. The program is also done in conjunction with Bloomberg Philanthropies and Babson College. I highly recommend applying if you are a business owner or leader.

In Baltimore, I was surrounded by a group of CEOs in that day's course of networking. My task in class was to write down on the "Mapping Your Network Worksheet" my "Opportunity Statement" for my existing company, Enradius. The goal was to find someone in your network of contacts, "who you know," that can help you. I wanted to hire a sales rep in Pittsburgh, and all I could drum up in my head was buying a LinkedIn or Indeed recruitment ad. My mind was mush; I didn't know how to connect the dots with my network, much less do it through social media, without paying for it.

So here I am—I've been in business for decades, have gone to thousands of networking events, and know thousands of people, but I didn't have one connection to a person in Pittsburgh who might be a good candidate for a sales position. So being that person who always thinks, "What's the worst that could happen?" I raised my hand in class and asked the group for help. No question is dumb, right? Well I sort of felt dumb since I'm supposed to be a CEO and a marketing/sales guy with expertise, but I had to lead with being a little vulnerable.

Lo and behold, a classmate responded. Gary Ditto, who runs a successful staffing company, said, "You should connect with our mutual friend Jodi, since she's from Pittsburgh and she might be able to connect you with her network out there." I was dumbfounded. It was right in front of me, and it was something so simple. This wasn't just regular networking; this was what I termed Needworking. I had a Need that Needed to be fulfilled, and it all made logical sense after the fact.

I feel that sometimes we are moving so fast in the day-to-day craziness that we don't see things clearly right in front of us. We all have Needs, and we can't always take care of them by ourselves. We Need others to help, and there's a complete sense of self when we are helping others. The concept of Needworking filled my head, and I went online during class and was shocked to see that the domain name was available. Cha-ching! I bought it. I had plans for this one, unlike the other hundred domains that I have conjured up, like HumaneStore.com, SinkSalts.com, Closetflippers.com, datagrow. com, and oceancity.fun, which have mostly collected dust. This one was different, though. I had a good feeling about it, and then all hell broke loose.

In 2020 we were all affected by the Covid-19 pandemic, the lockdowns, the political anger, and people getting sick. I wasn't immune from the devastating effects of Covid-19. My father caught it, very soon after he had his gallbladder removed, and while he was recovering from the surgery, it took hold and wouldn't let go. It was so painful to not be able to be by his side while he was in the ICU on a ventilator. We had to watch him decline and succumb to the virus via FaceTime. It was heart-wrenching and painful and yet it gave me strength. My father would have given the shirt off his back to anyone. My parents had very little money, yet he was always donating to charities because he was grateful for everything he had and felt others Needed it more than he did.

In the aftermath of that experience, I decided to make Needworking a living, breathing process and product and use the inspiration of my father's spirit to make it my mission to help others with the knowledge and connections I've made throughout my career.

What is Needworking to me? Needworking is a psychologically safe place for people to find Trusted Allies, connect equitably in groups, or discover curated networking events to help further their individual goals and Needs.

In his book *The 7 Habits of Highly Effective People*, Stephen Covey discussed how we are interdependent: "Interdependence is the paradigm of we—we can do it; we can cooperate; we can combine our talents and abilities and create something greater together."

When I read this, it reminded me of the old Coca-Cola commercial where a culturally diverse group of young people is on a hilltop singing in harmony. That's my vision for Needworking: helping and showing people how to connect off of very simple principles, topics and Needs that we have in common. Needworking is bringing that commonality together.

Throughout the book you will notice that I've capitalized the word "Need." I know it's not typically capitalized in the middle of a sentence, but I felt the Need to use this style throughout the book. I challenge you to count how many times you say the word "Need" in a day. Millions of people around the world are saying the word "Need" as you read this. Needs are natural, and millions are seeking to fulfill their Needs.

Not everyone wants to ask others for help, but it is known that giving back is powerful. There are scientific studies done on the power of giving back, and we will explore some of these theories. I have spent a lifetime reading, researching, exploring, and learning about people and connecting. This book is a culmination of those experiences intertwined with this process I call Needworking. I will refer to many of the books I have read that have helped me fine-tune my networking skills. There are so many brilliant authors who have centered their lives and business around networking, and I think their findings are fascinating. I will share quotes from many of the writings I felt impacted my approach. In the end, the power of Needworking isn't so much the techniques of networking—it's in people's resilience to continue to connect and their willingness and kindness to help others. I have also quoted many of the people who have been using our Needworking platform on a regular basis.

Another thing you will notice woven throughout the book is inspirational quotes. I'm a sucker for quotes that have empowered people for generations. We post life quotes on the Needworking platform as well as on our social media channels. Who doesn't love a good quote? To get you started, here are a few:

"I have found that among its other benefits, giving liberates the soul of the giver."
MAYA ANGELOU

"The meaning of life is to find your gift. The purpose of life is to give it away."
PABLO PICASSO

> "It is every man's obligation to put back
> into the world at least the equivalent
> of what he takes out of it."
>
> **ALBERT EINSTEIN**

I'm not the expert on these things; I'm just the implementer based on what brilliant people have been saying for centuries. They each have a common theme of giving back to humanity, as we all should. This is what I term Needworking. It's the power of giving back to others based on what you have gained from your time being on this planet.

I also consume a lot of business books. I have loved soaking up knowledge since I was a teenager. So many of the business books I've read or listened to lately have been written around the stories of WeWork, Uber, Apple, and Amazon. However, that is the last time you will see those brands in this book. This book isn't about other businesses and how they started. This is about you. It's about sharing my experiences and my learnings and my concepts with you.

One of the best books I've read, multiple times, I might add, is *Superconnector: Stop Networking and Start Building Business Relationships that Matter* by Scott Gerber and Ryan Paugh. The first chapter, "The End of Networking," is one of the best-stated arguments for how we as a community should look at Networking. I am a superconnector, and I'm surrounded by superconnectors as the company I keep. I fully agree with Gerber and Paugh's belief that we Need to stop networking and instead become superconnectors. Social media has really hurt the way we have collaborated with others, because it promotes building followers and pushes professionals to create audiences. Gerber and Paugh are totally on point when they write: "'Networking,' as we know it, as we have been taught, is dead." The authors want to abolish the term and call it "connecting" instead. I couldn't agree more.

Needless to say, I came up with something I call Needworking, and it's based on the ideas of many thought leaders who believe that helping one another is the key to success. It's not being Needy, but we all have Needs. I feel we should revise the old quote, "It's not who you know; it's who knows you." The problem with this quote and what's happening to social media platforms today is people's desire to be known and to collect followers. Every creator wants to be known, and they keep pushing more content and showing more cleavage, dance moves, or workout videos. That may get them clicks and followers, but real relationships aren't being built.

What if we revised that quote to say, "It's not who you know; it's what you do for someone you may or may not know." Humans are resilient and have often come together in powerful ways, whether it's rebuilding a community after a tragedy or natural disaster has occurred, or simply giving advice to and empowering someone else.

I might be an older entrepreneur, but I wouldn't be where I am without wanting to know, and the Need to understand more. You learn a little bit along the way from everyone you meet or get to know. On my journey, the one thing I have done well is network with others. I hope by putting this concept of Needworking out there, you get to know me a little better, and I'm happy to help you with your journey, no matter how big or small it is.

CHAPTER 1

PUT IT DOWN ON PAPER

In 2018 when I thought up the Needworking name, I thought it was clever and exciting that no one had ever coined that term before. Months later I did some online searching for the term Needworking, and a YouTube video eventually reared its ugly head. Mark Murphy from Leadership IQ did a presentation that spoke to how handing out business cards and asking people for a job was not working. He noted, "It's Networking, not Needworking. Needworking is when you are talking to other people to get stuff from them."

How could this be? My great name and idea that everyone has a Need and we all have to help one another had just gotten the ol' kibosh by an online video dismantling the name and the process I had dreamt up.

I thought long and hard about this and decided to challenge that thinking. I do agree with his theory in principle, namely that you can't keep asking someone without giving something in return and networking isn't just handing out cards, but I believe every single one of us has a Need. No matter how big or small they are, we have

Needs. Needs to learn, Needs to acquire new business, Needs to earn a living. You shouldn't show up at a networking event online or in person without a goal or a Need in mind. People are there to help, so I have to challenge Murphy's thinking on how Networking is done.

I have to give credit to Scripps Television and their management training program that had the mantra "Challenge the Process." That was something I excelled at. I was so good at challenging their internal processes on digital marketing that Scripps asked me to leave. I felt the product wasn't as good as it could be, and the cost was too high for clients. I'm grateful for that opportunity to move my career in a different direction. I was able to start my own company after being let go. My current company, Enradius, runs marketing campaigns for various clients in several cities across the country.

At that moment in time, though, I was sure as hell Needy. I was out of work, had two kids, and had to reach out to my network to find another opportunity. Out of desperation, you find strength and resilience. I created my own opportunity and had to learn by doing and asking. I couldn't have done it without the support and belief of those first several clients.

The same thinking goes for this new concept of Needworking and the online platform of the same name. It's in the beginning stages, and I'm learning and growing it daily. The two main mantras I've lived by since my teen years are: 1) True wisdom is knowing you know nothing (Socrates), and 2) What's the worst thing that can happen if you ask? Learning and asking are just the way I've done things. It's not an exact science, and sometimes I do feel Needy asking people for help. I had to ask people about the concept; I set up surveys to determine viability, and I had to create nondisclosure agreements and send them off to the original platform members. There was a lot on my plate to get the idea off the ground, but the first thing I Needed to do was concept it and make sure there was a product market fit. You can't do things like this alone; you Need help from others.

The first thing I did was register the domain name and then check with the United States Patent and Trademark Office (USPTO) to make sure Needworking wasn't already protected, and it wasn't. I was free to craft my thoughts on what the concept of Needworking looked like and create the brand. It was time to "napkin it."

During a recent flight on Southwest Airlines, one of their cocktail napkins caught my attention: "Southwest Airlines was born on a napkin in 1971." The design had a simple triangle with three pinpoints: Dallas, Houston, and San Antonio. I have come up with so many ideas in my lifetime, but the ones that mean the most, I had to take the time to write them down. It was usually sketched on the closest thing I could find. Ideas, products, and companies are crafted daily on a piece of scratch paper or a cocktail napkin.

The idea for "Shark Week" as seen on The Discovery Channel was supposedly conceived in the mid-1980s during a brainstorming session at a bar. According to an article in *The Atlantic*, Shark Week's executive producer, Brooke Runnette, stated that the idea behind this cult phenomenon "was definitely scribbled down on the back of a cocktail napkin."

Oscar-winning screenwriter Aaron Sorkin also says he wrote *A Few Good Men*, the play that would become his first movie, on cocktail napkins when he worked as a bartender at a Broadway theater during a production of *La Cage aux Folles*.

When you have that brainstorm idea, here are three things you should do to see if it's a viable concept or name:

1. Google the name or idea to see if it might already exist and how your idea stands out from the competition.
2. Check to see if there is an appropriate domain name that you can acquire for the idea. I was shocked to see that Needworking.com was available, and I snatched it up right at that moment while I continued to work on the idea.
3. Check the United States Patent and Trademark Office online (USPTO.gov) to make sure your name or idea isn't protected. You should engage the help of a trademark attorney if you believe your concept or idea is available.

That Southwest cocktail napkin was a good reminder of how it all started and where it is now. Not all ideas come to fruition, but the true gift is the time you've spent exploring new ideas and then cementing that great idea in your brain and eventually turning it into something that can be shared with others when the time is right.

The concept of Needworking was spinning in my head. If I hadn't known Gary, how would I have found that person in Pittsburgh? Every social media platform out there clusters you with people you know or are connected with. This makes sense because we can relate to the people we know and trust, but the problem with social media is compounding. That's something the famed financial guru Warren Buffet loves in money, but in social media, compounding too many people and their activities can clutter our feed.

I thought, "How could others help and respond to your activities/needs?"

What most social media doesn't typically do nowadays is what the chatrooms and forums did in the past. The general concept of Needworking is to connect people in Topic-related posts and categories like Reddit, but meant more for business professionals and nonprofits.

I had this in my head, but I Needed to put it on paper. At this point it wasn't a project scope—it was more like a bucket list of what I wanted. Actually, let's call it a "Mountain List." A bucket list is actually a little depressing. Create a list of things to do before you die, or kick the bucket, as they say.

This is a life journey we are on, not a death journey. Let's term it something new, like the Mountain List. Before you plan to climb any mountain, you Need to prepare. I knew I Needed more than a napkin to plan out the Needworking concept. I Needed to create a list of features and functionality to ideally plot out what was in my head.

The Needworking concept Needed to accomplish several things for the user as I dreamt it:

1. It was all centered on a Need and the response, The reciprocity of people willing to help one another.

2. The announcement of Needs should not just go to people you know; it should extend to people who are experts in their industry.

3. It Needed to help people discover networking events in and around a geographic region or based on a Topic.

4. It Needed to bring people together based on similarities and finding ways to connect based on interests.

5. It had to be inclusive and not based on who you usually surround yourself with. Our shared experiences will only help us grow together.

6. It Needed to be engaging and have people keep coming back by gamifying and tallying actions on the platform.

7. It had to be different from LinkedIn, Facebook, Event-brite, Medium, and Quora, but use their best parts to enable our system.

I believed three strategies helped formulate what I wanted to create based on learned experiences.

➡ The curriculum of the 10K Small Businesses Program was crafted by Babson College, and I felt that they did a great job aligning the topics of the coursework, and we used it as a starting point for our Needworking site. We incorporated some of their categories and methodologies as the principal baseline to help connect my 10K group (thirty to forty members) and other groups similar to ours.

➡ I also felt that you can't have Needworking without addressing Maslow's hierarchy of Needs. This would be the foundation for the whole project. Maslow believed that reciprocity was actually at the top of the hierarchy, not self-actualization as he once theorized. More on Maslow later.

➡ Dunbar's number. Having too many connections can be a detriment and an easy way to get internet overload. I wanted to simplify how you connect with an ally. I mapped out all the topics I felt that people would connect on instead of just hashtagging; the system would build your feed based on the topics you choose. It's a process that will continually grow and expand as we keep the momentum building.

Here are just a few of the topics I started with, developed from the Babson business curriculum:

Accounting

Advertising

Banking

Benefits

Diversity

Education

Employment

Entrepreneurship

Equipment

Events

Exit Strategies

Finance

Gifting

Goals

Growth

Headspace

Human Resources

Legal

I didn't plan on growing the number of topics, but as our audience grew larger, many have requested additional topics they would like to see.

After writing an initial business plan and Mountain List, I then tried to diagram it on a PowerPoint presentation. Technically I couldn't build this project myself; as I mentioned earlier, I am the creative type and not the process or programming person. I don't have the focus Needed for that. Just writing this book was a challenge in and of itself. I Needed someone to help build out this website design from what was in my head and now on paper. I brought in a group of developers, one of whom I had met years earlier and kept in contact with. Had it not been for Ali and his team, this project would never have become a reality. I have heard so many positive comments on the ease of use of the Needworking platform and keeping the look and feel clean.

I still get excited every day about the page views and user growth, and especially how people are helping one another. It's working even better than we envisioned it in the beginning.

A funny sidenote about my Needworking idea. At my 10K Small Business graduation, I recall walking up to one of the Goldman Sachs executives and telling him about the brainstorm idea I had for connecting people. I was so excited because it not only stemmed from Maslow's hierarchy of Needs but also from the course I had just spent months in, and they also had invested in me. He said, "We already have an app for our 10KSB cohorts that they are completing." It took the wind out of my sails, but I am resilient and I decided it would not burst my bubble. I'm still determined to get Goldman Sachs involved in this project. It's on my Mountain List.

→ The Takeaway:

Putting your goals on paper is a powerful step towards turning your ideas into reality. Just like Southwest Airlines and Shark Week were born from simple napkin sketches, your idea could sprout the same way if you take the time to write down your ideas and aspirations. Create your own Mountain List and outline the features and functionality of your concept. Writing down your goals not only clarifies your vision but also helps you take the necessary steps to bring them to fruition.

CHAPTER 2

IT'S THE CLIMB

What is the mountain, and what are your tools?

Let's face it—we have all failed at some point in our lives. What is it that keeps you striving for more and not giving up? Have you ever felt vulnerable, yet empowered? If you haven't yet read Brené Brown's books, I hope you do. She is on the forefront of studying and researching vulnerability, advising fans and followers to share their feelings and put things out there. In her books *Daring Greatly* and *Rising Strong*, I love how she retold the story of Theodore Roosevelt's "The Man in the Arena" speech delivered at the Sorbonne, in Paris, France, on April 23, 1910. Brown's point is that we are all in our own arenas fighting. We fight and we struggle every day. Do we face it head on, or do we disappear and run? We have that fight-or-flight mentality, and lately I've been doing a little of both. Sometimes hiding is a way to reengage with yourself to know that things won't always be perfect, but you can't give up.

Brené Brown's 3 R's are something I Need to work on. For example, I have come to the realization that I am in one of these stages of the process at this very moment:

➜ **The Reckoning**
➜ **The Rumble**
➜ **The Revolution**

Right now I'm in my truth, my Reckoning.

I have a huge video game addiction. I love *Apex Legends*. That is a core time suck of my life. If I weren't writing this book, I'd be gaming and calling it my hobby. The game has everything I Need. It has challenges that keep me playing for maybe eighteen hours straight to beat them. I'm a superhero fan, and the Apex characters they have created with all of their special skills keep me engaged. Finally, I can get out of my head, out of the real world, when something isn't going my way, and I completely withdraw from real life and get sucked into this alternative world. The best part is when you are completely in stride with your random trio and you strategically defeat nineteen other teams in the game to become the champion. I like winning and meeting those challenges.

That's the lie I tell myself.

In reality, playing the video game has kept me away from spending time with my family, my companies, and just real-life problems I have to face. It's not the best place to be to move forward and ahead. It's an addiction, like alcoholism or overeating. It's a way of avoiding the reality so that you aren't facing the day-to-day.

My gamer name is Needworking. It's the way I get to justify playing hours on end. I call it "marketing." There is no justification, really, since 90% of the kids I'm playing with are just that. I'm maybe two to three times their age, and they have no idea they are playing with an old guy who started a networking platform.

I was speaking to an online teammate the other evening who was salty to me, and I told him to relax and mentioned that he was probably younger than my daughter. They don't know how to even comprehend a statement like that. They chuckle and think I'm a kid lying to them and then they realize, wait, this guy might be telling the truth. It's a little weirdly satisfying that you can mess with some of these cocky gamers. There are some tremendous players. I do pretty well, but I'm not at an elite level. They are the rulers of this world and it's their domain. They come from all walks of life: kids, students, dads with crying kids in the background—I've played with mom and son teams Many are on Twitch TV trying to make money just for their gaming skills. I'm sure Needworking has joined a Twitch channel or two. So if you play *Apex* and happen to read this book, now you know.

Playing these games is just a time suck; they pull you away from life goals and tasks—things you could be focusing on to be more productive. The game makers are brilliant at developing achievements to hit and incentives. Are you really conquering your world by conquering whoever is in the video games? I have created my own version of a goal list to combat the online habit and work on real-life milestones. It's called my Mountain List, and I describe the concept of the Mountain List later in this chapter.

The other thing I'm going to open up about is how mentally draining creating a new idea or business is. It takes every ounce of your heart and soul, and you have to beg, steal, or borrow to get ahead. If you see someone who has started their own business, take the time to speak with them. Yes, they are selling you something, but they have gone through the struggle to start something that isn't associated with a large corporation, and they more likely than most to have the weight of the world on their shoulders. I started my company eight years ago and took a massive pay cut. I admire every small business owner in the world who has gone out and actually done it. It's not easy. It's one of the most difficult things anyone can do. You have to jump off a cliff without a steady paycheck and make something work out of nothing. It is so rewarding to be a part of something that you have built yourself, but I could have taken an easier road with having a steady, higher-paying job at that as well.

It's hard, and sometimes you just want to run away and hide from it. Maybe it's why you might lose yourself in a video game.

We all have our mountains to climb, whether that's personal or professional or both. Writing this book is a climb, paying your rent or mortgage is a climb. How are you planning to get this done, and what tools do you require for the climb?

I tell myself, "You have a mountain to climb today." What does that climb look like?

To me, Needworking is my Mount Everest right now. It's the tallest peak I have to scale, and I have put the most planning and effort into something I don't know if I'll ever reach.

Don't get me wrong—I've done some pretty cool things in my life and have had so many random amazing encounters, have built a small company, and have been able to support people and their families, but it's draining. I really feel that this Needworking concept and this way of networking is enhancing collaboration.

I watched my father pass away from Covid-19, and part of me knows he couldn't fight any more. This man had a stroke at the age of forty-four and lost all mobility in his left arm and his feeling in his left leg. He lived for another thirty-four years, putting on clothes with the use of only half of his body. He would get stares and people feeling sorry for him and children looking at him as if he wasn't normal. He would also get people who were completely amazed by his determination and kind, loving heart when they met him. He loved life and loved his family, but struggled every day.

He is my inspiration. He would do the grocery shopping for the family because my mom had dementia, and she didn't know how to get from one part of the house to the next. He paid the bills and he took her to all of her medical appointments. He was a saint. He gave to charities, and he would talk and tell stories to everyone. He was a ball of love!

Here are the crappy things that would happen to him that people didn't see. He would fall in the street because his leg would get caught walking the dog. Because of his mobility problems, he would sometimes sit there with the dog for an hour until a neighbor or my brother Mike could help. My mom couldn't keep track of time that well and wouldn't think twice about where he was and definitely wouldn't have been able to help him up.

He was working at Food Lion to make extra money and because he just loved to work, wanted to meet people, and didn't know how to use a computer. He wanted to work in person and not online. My dad had worked in the food industry for years; it was in his DNA. He worked at Del Monte and many food distributors and was a legendary salesperson in Baltimore. The Food Lion near his house was the closest thing to get him back to those days. The manager who originally hired him left, and the new guy didn't want the handicapped man working there any longer. My father was fired for stealing. That's right; a man who gave to charity, went to church, and never stole a thing in his life was fired because of theft. He didn't have money with him in the store, so he limped out to the car to get his wallet, and he had a package of lunch meat in his mouth. Yes, he used to carry things in his mouth because he couldn't use his left arm.

When he got back into the store to pay, he was fired. I was furious. I called the store manager and lit him a new one, and his response to me was, "Your dad didn't fit in with the rest of the employees." It was mind-numbing. First off, that a human being would do that, and then second, that the moron actually told me he fired him based on discrimination. I still go to that Food Lion because it's closest to the house, and it still pains me to know how that man hurt my father and made him feel like a thief.

My dad tried to find other jobs after that, but companies really don't want the liability of hiring someone who might slip and fall and cause them to have to pay an insurance claim. My father wasn't one to sue, it wasn't in his nature; he just wanted to share his spirit with everyone else and support his family.

No one wants a legacy to be that of someone who was fired for stealing. No one thought of him that way—he put that pressure on himself, and it cost him physically because of his emotional state. He was in constant struggle and always wanted to succeed. That is why mental health is a topic on the Needworking platform. If you feel something, say something to others.

I often think I should have just had my father on the speaking circuit and created content for him because he could lift up a room. He was a proud member of Toastmasters and inspired many by his will to succeed.

I remember coming into the rehab center and watching my father doing physical therapy. The new therapist took one look at his limp arm and braced leg and didn't think he could climb up a set of stairs and then get back down. My father looked at him and said,

"That's nothing." He shocked the therapist by scaling up the stairs and back down. Stairs and climbs challenged him for decades, and he never gave up. That was his climb.

In 2014 I went to an *Inc. Magazine* Grow Your Company Conference (Growco) event that inspired me to shift from the corporate world and set off on my own to start my own company. The event was in Nashville and featured speakers like Mark Cuban, Jason Fried of Basecamp, Bert Jacobs from Life is Good, and many others. The fun part was the Nashville music, and Big Machine Records had country recording artists play the event, many of them just launching their careers. Justin Moore played, and I got to meet and get a picture with Joe Don Rooney from Rascal Flatts. Yes, I was geeking out, since they are a favorite band of mine.

They also had the singer-songwriter Jessi Alexander there. You may know the Miley Cyrus recording of "It's The Climb," but it was co-written by Jessi with Jon Mabe, and Jessi performed it there for the group. That was my moment, hearing Mark Cuban saying stop being a "wantreprenuer" and do it full time and then the words that Jessi has written. The song empowered me then and inspires me to this day. Just Google the song lyrics and soak them in.

Sometimes I lose my faith and I doubt myself. I doubt the idea of Needworking. Sometimes it's due to moments like the Kickstarter campaign I launched to beg for money for this project. My goal was $15,000, and in the first three days I successfully raised $2. It makes me doubt what I am doing, but that's balanced by moments when I see that hundreds of people have visited the site in a 24-hour period and are using it as an alternative to other social media.

I was having a really bad emotional week in May 2022, maybe because it was the two-year anniversary of my father's passing.

Needworking had been rejected by Snap's Accelerator, Baltimore's ETC Accelerator, Lighthouse Labs in Richmond, and Tech Crunch's Accelerator. It's just so time-consuming to write and ask people for help on a project that isn't revenue positive and nowhere near making a profit. Social media and ad tech just aren't sexy anymore. It's a mental drain and it's depressing. So depressing that I don't want to leave the house and network in person and see people. I just want to put my headphones on and play *Apex* and forget about the world.

But go out into the world I must, so I was on the Amtrak to Philadelphia to go to Technical.ly's Philly Tech Week. All was quiet on the train, and then the door opened, and this loud tinny-sounding music was blaring to disrupt our peaceful train ride. It was the car attendant taking tickets, and as he got closer I could hear those words coming from the small speaker attached to his hip, "It's the climb." I just soaked it in, lost in deep thought. I knew that was my sign. This train, this trip. I was meant to be on it. I had to keep my faith.

I met some amazing people at the event and really feel good about the path those roads are leading me on.

My father was looking out for me that day. It's not only faith but a little luck of the Irish. That's why we chose green as our color for Needworking; it also represents go, move forward, proceed. So when you see a post on Needworking, don't just give it a "like"; give it a four-leaf clover in memory of James Carberry. He is my inspiration for always moving forward and always climbing.

So what is my point in all of this?

You Need the tools and possibly others to help you climb Everest or your daily mountains. Not just a basic hike or a trek, but a climb. Posting a Need and asking others for help along the way is something that is not out of the ordinary. Getting guidance or understanding how to achieve with someone's help is not only how we connect but how we learn to navigate a potentially rocky journey.

According to ClimbTallPeaks.com (https://climbtallpeaks.com/what-equipment-do-you-need-to-climb-a-mountain/), there are three types of climbing: rock climbing, ice climbing, and mountaineering.

> **Rock climbing:** Using your hands and feet to climb up a vertical rock surface. May or may not include an ascent to the summit of a mountain.

> **Ice climbing:** Using your hands and feet to climb up a vertical rock surface. May or may not include an ascent to the summit of a mountain.

> **Mountaineering:** Climbing with the goal of reaching the summit of a mountain. May include rock climbing or ice climbing or both. May sometimes be nontechnical and no extra equipment is required.

We are all mountaineering in life, and some Need more help than others climbing to their peaks. I had the opportunity to speak with Andrew Buerger, the author of *Carrying a Flag from Pain to Passion*. Andrew is a philanthropic mountain climber and has raised over a million dollars for the causes he supports with his incredible mountain journeys. He takes the lessons he's learned from climbing mountains like Mount Rainier and Mount Shasta and shares his stories speaking at events such as TEDx and also on his podcast *It's the Climb*.

One of Andy's lessons is about finding a guide. You can't climb up or down steep mountains without a guide. If you fall in a dangerous crevasse, it's a recovery, not a rescue. The guides point you in the right direction and help you to not get lost. In his TEDx talk, he asked the audience, "Who here likes asking for help?" No hands in the audience went up. Then he asked, "Who here likes helping people?" Everyone raised their hands.

Andy found a guide in Seth Goldman, the founder of Honest Tea and Just Ice Tea. Seth helped Andy take his organic protein smoothie company to the fifth-fastest-growing organic food company in 2016. It would never have happened without Andy asking someone to help him with his Need.

People will help you climb your mountains. You just have to plan accordingly and find someone who is willing to help and spend time with you. As was shown in Andy's TEDx talk, there's a room full of people who want to help and not many asking.

The more I think about creating Mountain Lists, it gets my adrenaline pumping and thinking about the Rocks (goals) I want to tackle. In his book *First Things First*, Stephen Covey talks about putting the Big Rocks first. You tackle the Big Rocks in steps because if you're only focused on the small stuff, the Big Rocks will never move.

I've modeled a ninety-day Mountain List at the end of this chapter, and as I mentioned in the Introduction, there are people you are connected with and even experts on Topics that can help you move the Big Rocks, whether it's personal or professional.

A Big Rock could be asking for a raise, saving money to go on a dream vacation, hiring a new employee, losing weight, or working on breaking an addiction. Rocks are heavy and we sometimes can't carry a rock on our own, so we Need help. The principles of Needworking, tapping your own network, and connecting with experts with insights are just the tools you Need to help you scale the mountain.

Now visualize those Big Rocks in a bucket. Buckets can split. Buckets are also what you use to mop the floors, put scraps in from odd jobs, scoop up yard debris, and yes, you can fill them with sand at the beach.

Turn that bucket upside down and it could look like a mountain and not just something you fill for the sake of filling it. The other thing I like about the Mountain List is that it resembles Maslow's hierarchy of Needs, and there is a peak to reach.

When my kids were younger, I asked them daily, "What was your peak of the day and what was your pit?" It gave me a sense of the good things and frustrating things that happened in their day. Their answers were thoughtful, and it forced them to respond that way. Just asking, "How was your day?" gave them the easy way out to simply say, "It was good."

The more I think about the Mountain List, the more I feel it blends into the idea of vision boards and reaches a higher level of accomplishment rather than just throwing something in a bucket.

I'm going to add one more thing to this planning sheet I call the Mountain List. You might have heard of a Big Hairy Audacious Goal (BHAG). I've heard plenty of people use this terminology and more recently was presented with it in a Scale Up Your Business group. It refers to a clear and compelling target that an organization tries to reach. The term was coined in the book *Built to Last: Successful Habits of Visionary Companies* by Jim Collins and Jerry Porras. The acronym BHAG is pronounced "bee hag."

Personally, I don't like it. First of all, BHAG reminds me of a witch and then you have to call her hairy? Let's flip my own thinking and call it the Apex Goal. I know, I know; I Need to stop thinking about *Apex Legends* and the time waster that it is, but what if I flip that narrative and spend more time on my own Apex Goals?

Ironically, "apex" means the highest point. If you think about the mountain you want to climb, sure, we climb the Big Rocks to get there, but where's there? What is the highest point? What is your peak? Your Apex Goal could be the goal you set for yourself for one month, one year, maybe even five years or more. What's your vision, and how does that Apex Goal fit into where you want to go or do next?

You can create your own daily, monthly, or yearly Mountain List by creating better habits and structure. Here are four books I highly recommend for people struggling with their focus and getting to the top of their mountain:

1. *The 7 Habits of Highly Effective People* by Stephen Covey:

➡ Effectiveness starts with understanding your own values and principles, and aligning your actions with them.

➡ Introduces the concept of "paradigm shifts" and encourages readers to adopt a proactive mindset rather than being reactive.

➡ Emphasizes the importance of interpersonal communication and developing win-win relationships.

➡ Introduces the concept of "sharpening the saw," which focuses on continuous self-improvement and personal growth.

2. *Atomic Habits* by James Clear:

➡ Emphasizes the power of small habits and incremental improvements in achieving long-term success.

➡ Introduces the idea of habit formation and provides practical strategies for building good habits and breaking bad ones.

→ Emphasizes the importance of understanding the cues, cravings, responses, and rewards that drive habit loops.

→ Encourages readers to focus on identity-based habits and align their habits with the person they want to become.

3. *Mastering The Rockefeller Habits* by Verne Harnish:

→ Provides a framework for scaling and growing businesses effectively.

→ Introduces the concept of "Rockefeller Habits," key principles for managing and growing a business.

→ Emphasizes the importance of setting and executing clear priorities, establishing a company's core values, and developing effective communication rhythms.

→ Provides practical tools and strategies for strategic planning, execution, and team alignment.

4. *The Mountain Is You* by Brianna Wiest:

→ Focuses on self-discovery and personal growth, encouraging readers to take responsibility for their lives and transform themselves.

→ Emphasizes the power of self-awareness and the importance of examining one's beliefs, emotions, and thought patterns.

→ Encourages readers to embrace vulnerability and face their fears in order to overcome obstacles and achieve personal fulfillment.

➜   Explores the concept of resilience and highlights the potential for growth that can arise from challenging experiences.

➜   Provides insights and practical tools for developing a positive mindset, practicing self-compassion, and creating a meaningful life.

Overall, these books provide valuable insights into personal effectiveness, habit formation, and business growth. They emphasize the significance of aligning actions with values, developing good habits, and implementing effective strategies for personal and professional success.

The mental and emotional toll of creating a new idea or business, or just living life, requires immense dedication, perseverance, and sacrifice. The personal story of my father's struggles and challenges serves as a powerful inspiration for me. Despite his physical limitations, he was a loving and determined individual who faced discrimination and hardships. Witnessing his strength and perseverance motivates me to continue my own climb.

The Takeaway

This chapter emphasizes the importance of acknowledging and confronting personal and professional challenges, while drawing inspiration from the resilience and determination of those who have faced their own mountains to climb. It's about staying strong, pushing forward, and embracing the journey, for it's in the climb that we find growth and fulfillment. Create your Mountain List and start today.

Your Mountain List

Needworking

Complete the form below with your target goals in mind for the next 30 days. Take **STEPS** - Simple, Timely, Efficient, Possible, Securable, activities to complete every 30 days. Once a goal is achieved, move to another priority goal for the next 30 days. Revisit the improved action area to ensure efficiency and improvements are maintained upon if necessary.

Day 1 Start Date – End Date		
30 Day Mountain Forecast	Potential Needworking Allies	
Big Rock 1:	Who Can Help?	Due Date (When)
STEPS TO ACHIEVE		
STEPS 1:		
STEPS 2:		
STEPS 3:		
Choose Topics to share your Rock with others		
Big Rock 2:	Who Can Help?	Due Date (When)
STEPS TO ACHIEVE		
STEPS 1:		
STEPS 2:		
STEPS 3:		
Choose Topics to share your Rocks with others		
Big Rock 3:	Who Can Help?	Due Date (When)
STEPS TO ACHIEVE		
STEPS 1:		
STEPS 2:		
STEPS 3:		
Choose Topics to share your Rocks with others		

What is Your Apex Goal? This is a long-term Vision Goal by Climbing the Big Rocks will help you scale and to get you to your highest point, The Apex.

_____ Target Date _____

When faced with a daunting rock, remember that it's not about its size, but the strength and courage you summon to ascend it. Embrace the climb and let each rock become a milestone in your journey, and don't be afraid to ask for help.

CHAPTER 3

NEEDWORKING AND THE HIERARCHY OF NEEDS

The name Needworking kept running through my head like a freight train. I couldn't stop thinking about it. What is Needworking? How do you define it? As Simon Sinek would say, "What is the Why"? (This is the question he poses in his book *Start with Why*.)

I started to really get deep into the question, What is truly a Need? We all have Needs. I remember how much I enjoyed taking psychology classes in college, and Maslow's hierarchy of Needs just intrigued me. The top of Maslow's pyramid was self-actualization, and if that's the case, we would always be learning about ourselves and adapting to those varying Needs we have in the various stages of our lives.

Those Needs transform us into the people we can become, and you can't do it alone. When you are an infant, let's face it; you require help. You can't survive on your own. Some of us Need more help than others.

I was one of those kids that Needed more help. I was put up for adoption when I was a baby and remained in the care of Catholic Charities until I was eighteen months old. I was too little to have any recollection of those days, and the sad part is, I had only one baby picture from when I was born. There were no other pictures of me until my adoptive parents brought me home. So I definitely had Needs that were beyond my control and beyond my ability to meet. The nuns cared for me, I Needed a place to stay, someone paid for that place, and then others had to find a suitable place for me to live. I am very grateful for just being here, and that others took care of me and raised me.

From the digging I did, I evidently was put into a foster home at around a year old, but my new father had lost his job and they had economic issues, so back I went. As I said, I don't recall any of that, but I do know it was a community that cared for me, and community makes the difference.

You have to surround yourself with people who will lift you up, and you in return can help them as well. It all comes back to the fact that we all have Needs, and the internet is full of cool ways to fulfill those Needs. We have services for every Need imaginable. For example, I used 23andMe and Ancestry.com to do a deeper dive on my "where do I come from" Need.

My inquisitiveness led me to finding four sisters and a brother that I wasn't aware of. It came at a perfect time at the start of a new year, after recently losing my parents.

Maslow's Hierarchy

Let's start by defining what Maslow's hierarchy is and how you can also use online tools and apps to fulfill the Needs he includes in his pyramid.

Physiological Needs

At the base of Maslow's hierarchy are physiological Needs that are essential to our survival. Some examples include:

- ➤ Food
- ➤ Water
- ➤ Breathing
- ➤ Shelter
- ➤ Clothing

Aside from the breathing part, everything that you Need, you can get through an app. Shelter from Rent.com or Airbnb. Food from DoorDash or Grubhub. Clothing from a million places. Life has changed so drastically in the last twenty years because of the ability to fulfill our Needs faster. For those who are economically challenged and/or who have limited access to the internet and basic resources, it might take more time to discover places where they can get what they Need.

Security and Safety Needs

As we climb the levels of Maslow's hierarchy, the Needs begin to be a little more complex. People want to protect themselves and their health, so they begin to prepare and plan for these behavioral components. Some of the basic security and safety Needs include:

➔ Financial security, including finding a job

➔ Health and wellness

➔ Safety against accidents and injury

➔ Finding a home in a safe neighborhood

Together, the safety and physiological levels of Maslow's hierarchy of Needs are often referred to as "basic Needs." Again, these Needs can be fulfilled by apps like Zillow, WebMD, Headspace, Calm, Fitbit, The Zebra, Jerry, Indeed, E*TRADE, and OpenSea. Of course, companies that you already deal with likely have their own portals, so you can check your statements and levels of financial well-being.

Social Needs

Social Needs include belonging, acceptance, and love. The Need for emotional relationships and connection drives our human behavior. Some of the things that satisfy this Need include:

➔ Friendships

➔ Romantic attachments

➔ Family

➔ Social groups

➔ Community groups

➔ Religious organizations

Groups and communities also play a huge role in how you express yourself and grow that sense of belonging with others.

Offline and online, you probably belong to many groups and communities, including religious groups, sports teams, chambers of commerce, and neighborhood book clubs. There are plenty of ways online to connect with groups: Nextdoor, Your Chamber websites, Slack, Twitch, YouTube, Twitter, Microsoft Teams, and of course Facebook. When we first launched Needworking, we didn't have a groups feature, but we realized that LinkedIn groups might have millions of people, and they just get overloaded with too many "takers" in their communities. We decided to add groups to our platform and will dive into Needworking groups in a later chapter.

Esteem Needs

Esteem Needs are the psychological Needs of the hierarchy. Most humans want to be appreciated, respected, or just plain given attention. At this level, esteem Needs begin to play an important part in motivating behavior and adaptability in our cultures, wherever that might be.

It is truly amazing seeing people who are just regular humans doing things online and growing audience levels that haven't been seen since there were only three television networks. Populations at that time were basically split by the decision to watch a program on one of the three networks, so television ratings for any individual program were astronomical due to limited choices. Now it is a different world where followers and fans can join anyone's Instagram or TikTok channels. At the time of this writing, the top TikTok artist, Charli D'Amelio (@charlidamelio), had 140 million followers. In comparison, talk show host Jimmy Fallon's Instagram has just 21 million followers, and his television audience averages 1.5 million viewers versus Johnny Carson, who had five times that viewership in the 1970s and '80s.

It seems like there are so many people trying to get others' attention to gain respect and appreciation. People Need to sense that they are valued by others and making a contribution to the world.

The apps and online platforms to see esteem Needs in action include TikTok, Instagram, Facebook Reels, YouTube, Vimeo, Discord, and LinkedIn. Needless to say, when people are projecting, dancing, lip-synching, or playing practical jokes on others, there really isn't a lot of two-way conversation happening. I call it "The Uncle Kracker Conundrum." Uncle Kracker had a huge hit single in 2001 called "Follow Me" that reached #5 in the Billboard charts. Our society has become the "Follow Me" culture.

You might have seen *The Truman Show*, a film starring Jim Carey as Truman Burbank, the unsuspecting star of "The Truman Show," a reality television program filmed 24/7 through thousands of hidden cameras and broadcast to a worldwide audience. Christof (portrayed by Ed Harris), the show's creator and executive producer, seeks to capture Truman's authentic emotions and give audiences a relatable everyman. Little did they know that this was what would become of millions of people across the planet (posting videos of snippets of their lives on various online platforms, voluntarily).

Our deeper connections with people and the level of intimacy we can achieve might be altered by this "show" that people are creating around themselves. Platforms like Medium or even podcasts open up the opportunity for a little more dialogue to understand that influencer more in depth, but can you build a true relationship and connection with that person on this level? Getting millions of followers or even hundreds just isn't what some people want do, and limiting your connections can be a little more advantageous, as well as difficult, and something we will dive into later.

There is a large percentage of the population now going through mental health issues because of social media, whether it's lack of self-esteem from bullying online or just not being able to maintain that follower base and continually having to be someone or something you are not. I imagine keeping up with content and a large audience can be draining. It's fascinating being a part of a culture of people posing in random places with a camera person in tow. It's become a common occurrence at events and exotic tourist locations. We have become a world full of online creators.

Self-Actualization Needs

At the very peak of the original version of Maslow's hierarchy are the self-actualization Needs. Maslow later modified his hierarchy. Self-actualized people are self-aware, concerned with personal growth. They are less concerned with the opinions of others and wholly interested in improving themselves and fulfilling their potential.

One of my mantras has always been, "True wisdom is knowing you know nothing at all." It was the voice in my head that kept me learning and growing and still does to this day. Albert Einstein once said, "When you stop learning you start dying." Your brain is a large muscle, and if you aren't challenging yourself, you lose something of yourself.

"What a man can be, he must be," Maslow explained, referring to the Need people have to reach that peak of their full potential. According to Maslow's definition of self-actualization, "It may be loosely described as the full use and exploitation of talents, capabilities, potentialities, etc. Such people seem to be fulfilling themselves and to be doing the best that they are capable of doing. They are people who have developed or are developing to the full stature of which they are capable."

The internet has opened up a huge opportunity for people to explore their own path to self-actualization: the realization of one's full potential and the pursuit of personal growth, creativity, and fulfill-ment. Here are some examples of self-actualization:

Creative Pursuits: Engaging in creative activities such as painting, writing, music composition, or other forms of artistic expression to channel one's inner thoughts and emotions.

Entrepreneurial Ventures: Starting and successfully running a business or project that aligns with one's passions and skills, allowing for innovation and personal fulfillment.

Personal Growth and Learning: Continuously seeking knowledge, whether through formal education, self-study, or experiential learning, to expand one's understanding of the world and oneself.

Spiritual Exploration: Deepening one's spiritual connec-tion through practices like meditation, mindfulness, and self-reflection, leading to a greater sense of purpose and inner peace.

Embracing Authenticity: Being true to oneself, accepting one's strengths and weaknesses, and living in alignment with personal values, regardless of societal expectations.

Physical Achievements: Pushing the boundaries of physical capabilities through activities like sports, outdoor adventures, or fitness challenges, fostering a sense of accomplishment and resilience.

Cultural Exploration: Immersing oneself in diverse cultures, languages, and experiences, gaining a broader perspective on life and developing an appreciation for global diversity.

Mind-Body Connection: Developing a strong mind-body connection through practices like yoga, tai chi, or meditation, enhancing self-awareness and overall well-being.

Overcoming Challenges: Successfully navigating personal challenges, setbacks, or adversities, and using these experiences to develop resilience, adaptability, and a stronger sense of self.

Continuous Self-Improvement: Setting and achieving personal goals, whether they're related to career, relationships, health, or other aspects of life, and consistently striving for self-improvement.

It's important to note that self-actualization is a subjective concept, and what represents self-actualization can vary widely from person to person. It's about finding what truly resonates with your individual values, interests, and aspirations and working towards realizing your unique potential.

In 1967 Abraham Maslow started to reconceptualize his hierarchy. He was nearing his sixties, and his health was beginning to fail. He rethought the notion that the peak of self-actualization was not the finalization of one's self. Once we reach that point of self-actualization, do we just shut it off and stop? He revised his hierarchy to have transcendence at the top, above self-actualization. Maslow stated, "The goal of identity [self-actualization] seems to be simultaneously an end-goal in itself, and also a transitional goal, a rite of passage, a step along the path to the transcendence of identity. If our goal is the Eastern one of ego-transcendence and obliteration, of leaving behind self-consciousness and self-observation, then it looks as if the best path to this goal for most people is via achieving identity, a strong real self, and via basic-Need-gratification."

Giving back after we have accomplished what we have set out to achieve is one of the greatest gifts you could ever give someone. Your knowledge, your time, the journey that you've lived should be passed down to others in their own journey.

After I developed the Needworking concept, I started consuming a tremendous number of books and was surprised to see how many authors had spoken about reciprocity and referred back to Maslow. In his books *7 Habits of Highly Effective People* and *First Things First*, Stephen Covey reflects back on Maslow and discusses a question he constantly poses in his teachings: "How many on their deathbed wish they spent more time in the office or watching TV?" The answer is no one. Covey later writes about his granddaughter Shannon helping orphans in Romania, and it resonated with me.

Years later I returned back to that orphanage in Baltimore, St. Vincent's Villa Maria, and I spent time sitting with the kids and serving them holiday meals. It was such an amazing thing to dig back down and discover where I came from, and hopefully I made a difference in some of the kids' lives. They were shocked when I told them I worked for the cool hip-hop radio station in town and that I was once a resident of their current home. It gave them hope. That experience meant so much to me that I invited friends and family to see the joys of helping make the holidays better for the kids at the facility, inviting them to walk in with even just a small donation of clothes. My kids and I made it an annual ritual to do this, and I was happy to share that experience. It's truly the joy of giving back and reciprocity.

Just as my family does, I am sure you have your own rituals of giving back. Some people just do it and don't think twice about it, and that's the way it should be. When you are giving something of yourself, you shouldn't expect anything in return. Good things will come to you by opening your heart, being a little vulnerable, and helping others. Look to your local community and volunteer at food banks, or give your time to a nonprofit organization. I'm on several committees myself.

There will be those who will see this on a bookshelf and completely ignore it because of the simple fact that they are takers or simply don't believe in a process to work with others and have a do-it-all-yourself attitude. The world is full of people like them. Adam Grant has done extensive research on the topic and lays it out in his book *Give and Take*.

In professional interactions, it turns out that most people operate as either takers, matchers, or givers. Whereas takers strive to get as much as possible from others and matchers aim to trade evenly, givers are the rare breed of people who contribute to others without expecting anything in return. These styles have a dramatic impact on success.

What are truly your needs right now? What can you do to help your situation at this very moment? Who are you going to share it with? Where do you start?

If you don't know where to turn, come visit Needworking. com and simply share a Need with our community. Make an ask! Depending on the Need and your Topic, we likely have people who can point you in the right direction.

Appreciate an Ask and the Needs of Others

I'd also recommend that you appreciate "The Ask." Gratitude and appreciation are the two biggest gifts you can give to someone, and it costs you nothing. Yes, you can buy them a thank-you card, but sending them a quick note via email or instant message shows that you took in that ask and it meant something. If someone takes the time to ask you for something personally, it means that you are well thought of as a person who could be willing to listen. People tend not to ask, so when they do, it means it's important to them, and you are important to them.

A person I've known for a few years recently asked to jump on a call and ask about Needworking. It means the world to me that someone took the time to want to find out more. If someone is asking you about your business or a situation, soak that in and don't take it for granted—especially at a networking event when everyone is buzzing around like bees to honey.

Your message or response can simply be a reflection of a meeting that happened or a specific ask. It doesn't have to be so complicated, either. It could be something as simple as, "Thank you for asking about Needworking—I really appreciate it. It's been a hard journey starting something new, and you reaching out to me personally meant a lot to me. Have a great week!"

Complete strangers can also impact the course of your journey. I was at a conference for Maryland Nonprofits. They have an annual conference for their nonprofit organizations who are members, and have various sessions and speakers. Speakers will provide knowledge of the industry and help educate others at these conferences, and it's a great opportunity to connect with other professionals interested in a specific topic. On that day I met Viola, who stopped at our Needworking booth to ask what we did. I told her my story about my father passing away from Covid, and I wanted to change the way people connect and help nonprofits.

She looked at me and apologized in advance and started to tear up. She started telling me how amazing I was writing a book and creating this platform and that my father is looking down on me so proud. I was overwhelmed and choked up. In a world full of people who are so busy trying to get your attention, that connection and those powerful words from a stranger sunk deep in my soul. She listened and was so vulnerable, something I wasn't expecting that day.

You remember those moments when parents tell you they are proud of you, but when someone drops all of their professional defenses and gets so deep and passionate about what you have created, it is a moment of awakening at the deepest level of connection. I instantly considered Viola as a trusted Ally on my journey, and it was with a twenty minute conversation that had profound meaning to me. What's even more amazing is that she had just graduated from college and was Valedictorian of Psychology. Hopefully there will be opportunities that I can share with Viola and impact her journey as much as she did for me.

The Takeaway

Everyone has Needs. It's only natural, but sometimes we don't know where or who to turn to for help. Sometimes it's the power of ourselves, and other times it's the power of a network.

Abraham Maslow proposed the hierarchy of Needs, which highlights the different levels of Needs that individuals strive to fulfill. Near the top of this hierarchy lies the Need for self-actualization, where individuals seek to reach their fullest potential and become the best version of themselves. Maslow's emphasis on self-actualization reminds us that every person possesses an inherent Need to grow, develop, and contribute in meaningful ways.

Self-actualization is not simply about achieving success or attaining external markers of accomplishment. It goes beyond that, encompassing the pursuit of personal fulfillment, authenticity, and the realization of one's unique talents and capabilities. Maslow describes self-actualized individuals as those who have reached the full stature of their potential, actively utilizing and exploring their skills, creativity, and capacities.

To embark on the journey of self-actualization and fulfill our potential, we Need to recognize and prioritize our Needs across the first five levels of Maslow's hierarchy. Each level builds upon the foundation of the previous one, and only when the lower Needs are reasonably satisfied can individuals focus on the higher ones.

Once these foundational Needs are reasonably fulfilled, we can dedicate ourselves to the pursuit of self-actualization. This journey is highly personal and unique for each individual. It involves introspection, self-reflection, and the exploration of one's passions, interests, and potentialities. To support this process, there are several resources available that can aid in fulfilling our Needs:

1. **Personal Development Books:** Books on personal growth and development can provide valuable insights, practical strategies, and inspiration to help us explore our potential and enhance our self-awareness.

2. **Mentors and Role Models:** Seeking guidance from mentors or looking up to inspirational role models can offer valuable perspectives, encouragement, and guidance along the path of self-actualization.

3. **Skill-Building Workshops and Courses:** Engaging in workshops and courses that align with our interests and aspirations can help us acquire new skills, enhance existing ones, and broaden our horizons.

4. **Supportive Communities:** Joining communities of like-minded individuals who share similar goals and interests can foster a sense of belonging, provide support, and create opportunities for collaboration and growth.

5. **Self-Reflection Practices:** Engaging in regular self-reflection through practices such as journaling, meditation, or mindfulness can promote self-awareness, clarify values, and facilitate personal growth.

By recognizing and fulfilling our Needs across Maslow's hierarchy, we lay the foundation for self-actualization and the pursuit of our highest potential. The journey towards self-actualization is ongoing and ever-evolving, as we continue to learn, grow, and develop throughout our lives. Embracing this process and utilizing the available resources can empower us to become the best versions of ourselves and lead a life of purpose, meaning, and fulfillment.

Self-actualization can intertwine with reciprocity, creating a fusion that I perceive as the true meaning behind what I term as "Needworking." This entails aiding others based on where you are in your self-actualization journey.

Relationships: Cultivating deep and meaningful connections with others, fostering healthy and supportive relationships that contribute to personal growth and emotional well-being.

Helping Others: Making a positive impact on the lives of others through mentoring, coaching, volunteering, or charitable work, deriving satisfaction from contributing to the well-being of others.

Social Change and Advocacy: Taking an active role in advocating for positive social change and contributing to causes that align with personal values, making a difference in the world.

In embracing the intricate dance between self-actualization and the principle of "Needworking," we embark on a profound journey of interconnectedness. As we ascend through Maslow's hierarchy, it becomes evident that our individual growth harmonizes with the betterment of those around us. So, as we strive to become the best versions of ourselves, let us not overlook the transformative influence we possess to uplift others. How might the synergy between self-actualization and reciprocity shape our pursuit of purpose? What unique insights and contributions emerge when our personal journey towards fulfillment intertwines with our commitment to aiding others? In essence, as we stand at the crossroads of self-discovery and societal impact, how could we envision "Needworking" reshaping our lives and the world we touch?

CHAPTER 4

WRITE AND DIG INTO YOUR NEEDS—BE CONCISE

When people ask me what Needworking is and what a Need is, it sometimes can be daunting to explain it. Here is one way I have explained what it is:

Most social media platforms are based on the principle of your network; it's who you know. On Needworking, our principle is what someone Needs. We match complete strangers based on their interests and categories, and the sequencing puts that Need in your Need Feed. So people are helping others without necessarily knowing them in advance.

That's when the questions start. Okay, what's a Need? Explain to me what people Need. What kinds of Needs are people putting in?

I also have said that Needworking is based on Maslow's principles and his hierarchy of Needs and that peak Need of reciprocity. (That's everything I just wrote about in the previous chapter; it's still hard to get that into an elevator pitch.) I have tried explaining this to lifelong friends, and they have been perplexed by it, especially the Maslow part. Early on, a brilliant friend of mine who works for Google took months to understand what it was I was trying to do. It just didn't compute, especially because my value proposition was all over the place. He later came back and said to me, "Now it makes sense—it's networking but when you Need to leverage someone else's network. A spin on LinkedIn but using your connection's extender contacts, hence Needworking."

I'm happy that he took the time to try to understand what was in my head. At that point, my Need really was to get people to relate and make sense and spend a little more time with me and my concept. We've had the platform live for over a year (at this writing), and people are using it and now understanding how it works as we improve the processes. People taking the time to give me feedback is one of the greatest gifts they could share. I am not going to be offended by anyone trying to help me improve my product and processes.

Kelly, my number one Needworking supporter, and I went down to South by Southwest (SXSW) in 2022 to see if we could make an impact and get some attention for Needworking there. SXSW is where so many of the "unicorns" went to get explosive growth and attention from investors and attendees alike. If you haven't seen *Super Pumped: The Battle for Uber* or *WeCrashed* (the story of the rise and fall of WeWork) here is the definition of a unicorn. "Unicorn" is the term used in the venture capital industry to describe a startup company with a value of over $1 billion and first coined by venture capitalist Aileen Lee in 2013.

We handed out T-shirts on the streets of Austin that said, "Kiss Me I'm Needworking." It was a fun way to garner attention and talk to people about the platform, especially because it was St. Patrick's Day. We have some fun pictures from the event on Instagram, and it gave us some great stories and feedback about Needworking.

The first realization was that we weren't ready for an event this big. We had nearly 1,000 shirts to distribute, just the two of us. It was exhausting, not to mention an expensive lesson, given the cost of travel, hotel, food, the event ticket, and the T-shirts. Our website wasn't ready because I don't think our development team completely understood our Need at the time to garner new sign-ups. We had one shot with our QR code and a landing page with a form that was just too complicated for SXSW attendees to fill out when they were in between sessions or heading to the next concert venue.

What we did learn was how people perceived the product and the process, and we had a lot of compliments and a lot of traffic to the site over the course of those days. We Needed to get some attention, and we Needed to do a market study, so we dug in deep to understand the market and the opportunity. One gentleman we bumped into in the hallway was from England, and when he saw we had arms overflowing with T-shirts, he asked for one. He wanted to know more about Needworking, and we explained it to him, and he said, "I get it, it's efficient networking." Kelly and I looked at each other and said, yes, that was it, one of the best ways to describe what we had set out to do.

If you think about some forms of in-person networking or even dating apps, it's a quick connection with no intimacy. You can swipe left or right to find a date for a night or a lifelong companion. The tools are there to do it; it just depends on your level of comfort.

When I attended the Goldman Sachs 10,000 Small Businesses program, they insisted that when we described our businesses we Needed to be concise. You have only a short time to be heard before you lose someone's attention. Asking someone for help, especially in a community you don't know, you Need to make certain your words are clear and you explain exactly what you Need help with and why it is important to you. Asking for help is not something you should be ashamed of, although many times we feel that we might inconvenience someone. "*Not* asking for help is one of the most self-limiting, self-constraining, even self-destructive decisions we can make," Wayne Baker writes in his book, *All You Have to Do is Ask*.

In their book *Superconnecter: Stop Networking and Start Building Relationships That Matter*, Scott Gerber and Ryan Pugh do an awesome job of breaking down deeper relationships and the importance of asking the right person, community, or resource. I highly recommend you read it because they share some extremely important principles, especially if you are just getting started being a "Superconnector." Just like the Goldman Sachs course, Gerber and Pugh stress the importance of being concise: "If you can't make it clear in thirty seconds what you are looking for and why in a simple, straightforward, and concise manner, don't say anything at all. You should lead with what you are trying to achieve—what the result you are looking for is and not the means by which you want to get there."

Honestly, their entire chapter "How to Make a Smart Ask" is powerful, and I truly believe you can follow their principles and connect with individuals you don't know and aren't already connected to. We built Needworking to not allow for thousands of followers or connections. Instead, we believe you should use our platform to form trusted, reliable connections. It's not a place where people are just trying to sell you something without building that relationship first.

One of the other ways I explain Needworking is simple, but it gets my point across. Have you ever heard of or done speed networking? The premise is you meet people in a room, and you quickly speak to one another for a limited amount of time, and then you are buzzed to do it again with a new person. Needless to say, that model, in a world full of instant gratification, is difficult if you really want to make deep connections. You end up with a stack of business cards and a lack of motivation to get back in touch with those people. Needworking is the complete opposite. It's essentially a way to really find out what a person Needs instead of just throwing a fast sales pitch out to everyone. Instead of speed networking, why not just have a general pitch session where everyone takes a turn standing up and presenting very briefly to the group?

Have you taken the time to ask someone else what they Need?

Knowing that I was working on Needworking, a friend of mine recommended a book by Susan McPherson, *The Lost Art of Connecting*. When I read her book, I felt instantly connected. Her book completely aligned with the vision I had for Needworking. Susan, like me, believes in being extremely proactive with your community. We introduced a simple Needworking Beta in March 2021, the same month she released her book. I was still mentally numb from my father passing away. I related to her personal story of her mom's tragedy, and it empowered me.

One of her chapters is titled, "How Can I Help?" Susan is one of those people who listens and offers help and suggestions to others and takes connecting to the next step. She writes, "Asking 'How can I help?' is an invitation for synergy. It sends the message: I am interested in what you do and who you are." Take it from me; she is. One of her other chapters is "Always Take (and Innovate on) the Meeting." So I was up to the challenge: I asked Susan for a meeting and got one. I know she was super busy with the launch of her book and other speaking appearances, but I felt special that she took the time out of her busy schedule to have a Zoom meeting with me.

As we develop more Needworking content, I'm excited about the potential to get Susan on another Zoom that is meant for our entire community.

A Dozen Ways to Make a Better "Ask"

In this realm of Needworking, where people come together to support and assist one another on shared topics, effective communication plays a pivotal role. Asking for help concisely is a skill that can facilitate meaningful collaboration and efficient problem-solving.

In the late '80s when I was in college and working for a radio station, I was planning on going to the Preakness Stakes in Baltimore. The Preakness is one of the three races in the Triple Crown of horse racing. Jim Slater, one of my co-workers at the station, said he was going as well. The challenge was how on earth we would find one another. This was before everyone had a cell phone, and there were nearly 100,000 people going to this event. What was the likelihood that we would be able to navigate that connection happening through the sea of people? Jim and I devised a plan, and it was with two popular characters of that time: Pee Wee Herman and his pig. I had a Pee Wee pull-string stuffed character that said "I know you are but what am I?", and Jim had the stuffed Pee Wee talking pig, Vance. Our mission was to unite Pee Wee and his pig by sourcing the crowd.

I navigated through the sea of people and asked dozens of people, "Have you seen Pee Wee's pig?", and Jim asked if anyone had seen Pee Wee. Somehow, it only took over an hour to find Vance in an infield of about 75,000 people without waving a decorated flag or the use of technology. It was simply asking other people for help, and they pointed us in the right direction. We both felt it was an amazing feat to make that happen in that short of a time frame.

Here are some guidelines on how to ask for help succinctly across a sample of topics we discussed in chapter 1. As mentioned, those topics are the connecting points of Needworking, and communicating your Need concisely is an important component of the process. I'm providing examples of concisely written Needs to illustrate the practical application of these principles:

1. **Understand the Topic:** Before reaching out for assistance, it is essential to have a clear understanding of the topic or issue at hand. Familiarize yourself with the basic concepts, terminologies, and relevant information related to the subject. This ensures that when you do ask for help, you can articulate your Needs more effectively.

2. **Identify the Specific Need:** Pinpoint the precise aspect of the topic that requires assistance. Narrow down your request to a specific question or problem to avoid overwhelming the person you're asking for help and to increase the chances of receiving a focused response.

3. **Be Direct and Clear:** When asking for help, be concise and straightforward in your communication. Clearly state your

request without unnecessary fluff or elaborate explanations. This approach saves time for both parties involved.

4. **Provide Relevant Context:** While being concise, it's crucial to offer enough context to help the person understand your situation. Share relevant details that are essential for them to provide meaningful assistance.

5. **Prioritize Key Information:** In cases where you have multiple Needs, prioritize them to ensure the most critical aspects are addressed first. This way, you maximize the chances of receiving prompt and effective assistance.

6. **Use Precise Language:** Choose your words carefully to convey your Needs accurately. Utilize industry-specific terms or jargon when appropriate, as this helps streamline communication and ensures that the person assisting you fully understands your requirements.

7. **Be Respectful of Others' Time:** When asking for help, remember to be considerate of the person's time and workload. Frame your request in a way that acknowledges their expertise while expressing gratitude for their assistance.

8. **Seek Specific Expertise:** If your Need falls within a specialized area, try to identify individuals or groups with the relevant expertise. This targeted approach enhances the likelihood of obtaining high-quality and tailored assistance.

9. **Utilize Available Resources:** Before seeking external help, leverage existing resources such as online forums, knowledge bases, or FAQs. This demonstrates your proactive approach and may lead you to find answers independently.

10. **Offer Reciprocity:** Needworking is a mutual endeavor, and it's important to foster a culture of reciprocity. Whenever

possible, express your willingness to help others in return or contribute to the community in a meaningful way.

11. **Be Open to Feedback:** When asking for help, be receptive to feedback and constructive criticism. Embrace diverse perspectives and be open-minded about different approaches to problem-solving.

12. **Express Gratitude:** Finally, remember to express gratitude to those who provide assistance. A simple thank-you goes a long way in building positive relationships and encouraging continued collaboration within the Needworking community.

Here are some simple examples of Needs based on Needworking Topic categories:

Accounting:

"Hi there! I'm currently working on an accounting project and Need some specific help with [specific thing—such as, how to handle a certain type of expense]—could you help?"

Advertising:

"Hi, I'm diving into advertising strategies [be specific] for my business and could use some guidance. Would you be open to sharing your insights on this specific advertising strategy or recommending any resources?"

Banking:

"I'm exploring different banking options for my new venture, and I was wondering if anyone had any recommendations or tips based on your experience in starting a banking relationship for my small business."

Benefits:

"I'm navigating the complexities of employee benefits, and I could really use some help understanding the various options available. Would someone be able to spare some time to discuss employee benefits with me?"

Employment:

"I'm in the process of searching for employment opportunities and was wondering if you have any advice on how to stand out in the job market or any networking connections that might be helpful in the field of [specific field]."

Looking for Employment:

"I'm actively looking for employment opportunities and would appreciate any leads or recommendations you might have in your professional network. I'm specifically interested in [specify industry or position]."

You can describe a concise Need on any of the platforms you are a member of. You have to decide which one is most appropriate for the concise Need you provide. On the Needworking platform, you can use the editing tool to include images, videos, or plain text, and mention/tag others. You can also choose a specific Topic that someone is following in their Need Feed.

On the Needworking platform, you can post and share it for anyone to see or someone that follows your tagged topic. You can post directly to your Allies/Trusted Allies or a Group you belong to. (More on these later.)

Here is an example of a concise post. This was a searchable post; I just typed "marketing" in the search bar, and it displayed as part of my Need Feed.

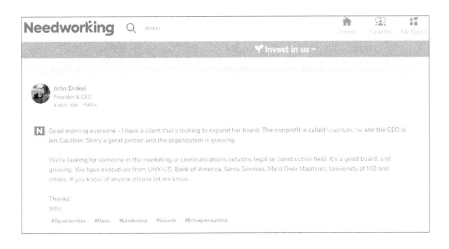

What's exciting is that John, the person who posted this Need, found and filled that board member role from someone on Needworking. I recently was invited to an event created on our platform by that same new board member. Congratulations, Sharon Mostyn! Sharon is probably the biggest giver on Needworking and has helped hundreds of people with her connections and knowledge. When you start adding your Allies like Sharon (more to come on that), you can see how many Needs and gives she has posted.

It's true, givers sometimes don't know what they Need. In many life-changing events we get stuck, and we Need help. I was speaking to a friend of mine about this whole concept of asking for help. She went through a life-changing event of getting a double mastectomy. There was the physiological trauma of having a potentially life threatening disease, the process of the surgery and body alteration, and then the recovery. She was working closely with a nurse practitioner who said people are going to say, "If you Need anything just let me know." So Kim was up to the challenge and listed everything that she needed, kids picked up and transported, coverage for clients at work, food preparation ideas, and many daily tasks that she wouldn't be able to do for weeks.

She put an idea in my head about the platform I just built. Why not create a private group in the system and list your needs and invite friends who have offered to help? We all rush around and don't take time for ourselves. In a situation as critical as Kim's, it's important to dig deep and understand your Needs and share them with others. You'll be amazed to see who comes to support you. You also have to be prepared to accept who doesn't.

The Takeaway

Mastering the art of asking concisely for help enhances your ability to tap into the collective knowledge and experience of others in Needworking. By understanding the topic, clearly expressing your Needs, and being respectful of others' time, you can foster fruitful collaborations and build a supportive network across various fields of interest. Embrace the principles outlined above and experience the power of effective Needworking firsthand.

CHAPTER 5

THE CORE 4 — GET YOUR NETWORKING TO SHIFT INTO G.E.A.R.

I have spent a tremendous amount of time researching and doing my own networking over the years. As many pieces as there are in networking, it really comes down to four core things you should be doing to build up your own personal network. I see the "Core 4" as a way of "shifting your networking into G.E.A.R."

The reason for shifting into G.E.A.R. is that sometimes we are not motivated enough to get out there and network. If you are motivated, you might not have a direction you want to move in. That's why I am recommending you remember and recall the Core 4 elements of building your networking principles and strategies:

1. Groups
2. Events
3. Allies
4. Reciprocity/Referrals

If you focus on building your network around these four core principles, it will help you fine-tune your networking strategies and also provide you with a psychologically safe place to concentrate on building your network.

The key to the Core 4 is your focus and what you specialize in. You are an expert in your field of knowledge, and you control your own destiny on how to navigate that field. Trust me, it can be like an asteroid field. You have to dart away, turn, pivot, get out of the way of flying rocks, and move forward to find the core group of people that you want to connect with.

I sat down with Andy Fulgham, one of the founders of the Two Twelve Referral Network in Richmond, Virginia. Andy and I discussed local networks and interconnecting with people who are connected to the members. Let's say a member could be a real estate agent or a graphic designer. You might not have a Need for either of those Topics at this moment, but they might be related to or connected to someone who is a Big Rock of yours, and the key is to ask.

Being in a safe group like this that passes referrals and connects in person regularly will build the trust to make that introduction and help build a stronger connection and your growing network.

Shifting into G.E.A.R. emphasizes the importance of motivation in networking. Often, individuals may lack the necessary drive to actively engage in networking activities. However, when motivation is present, individuals might struggle with determining the direction they want to move in. By recognizing this challenge, the theory of

Shifting into G.E.A.R. suggests that one should remember and recall the four core elements of networking principles and strategies.

The first core element, "Groups," refers to the importance of connecting with like-minded individuals who share similar professional or personal interests. Joining groups allows you to tap into collective knowledge, gain new perspectives, and establish valuable connections within your chosen field.

The second core element, "Events," highlights the significance of attending networking events. These events provide opportunities to meet new people, engage in conversations, and expand your network. By actively participating in events relevant to your industry or interests, you create a platform for meaningful interactions and potential collaborations.

The third core element, "Allies," emphasizes the importance of building mutually beneficial relationships with individuals who can support your networking endeavors. Allies can be mentors, colleagues, or industry experts who provide guidance, advice, and assistance in expanding your network and achieving your goals.

The fourth core element, "Reciprocity/Referrals," focuses on the value of giving and receiving support within your network. Networking is a two-way street, and by fostering an environment of reciprocity, you create a supportive ecosystem where individuals help one another and offer referrals, recommendations, and opportunities.

By consciously integrating these four core elements into your networking strategies, you can refine your approach and increase your chances of success. Understanding the significance of each element helps you prioritize and allocate your time and resources effectively, ensuring that you make the most out of your networking efforts.

Moreover, building your network around these core principles provides you with a psychologically safe space. It offers a supportive environment where you can concentrate on expanding your network without feeling overwhelmed or unsure of your direction. This psychological safety fosters confidence, motivation, and a sense of belonging within your network.

When you focus on groups, you surround yourself with individuals who share common interests and goals. This shared sense of purpose creates a nurturing environment where you can freely exchange ideas, seek advice, and collaborate on projects or initiatives.

Attending events aligned with your interests and industry exposes you to a diverse range of individuals who can offer fresh perspectives, valuable insights, and potential collaborations. By actively engaging in these events, you position yourself as an active participant within your professional community.

Cultivating Allies within your network is essential for personal and professional growth. Allies can provide mentorship, guidance, and support, helping you navigate challenges and seize opportunities. Building strong alliances contributes to the longevity and strength of your network.

Reciprocity and referrals are fundamental to establishing a mutually beneficial network. By actively seeking opportunities to support others and contribute to their success, you foster goodwill and create a network that is willing to reciprocate. Referrals from trusted connections can open doors to new opportunities and expand your reach.

In summary, the theory of Shifting in G.E.A.R. emphasizes the importance of motivation and direction in networking. By remembering and applying the four core elements of groups, events, Allies, and reciprocity/referrals, you can refine your networking strategies, establish a psychologically safe space, and build a strong and supportive network that contributes to your personal and professional growth.

We will dive into each of these in the following chapters, but I want to ensure that I repeat the Core 4 multiple times throughout the book. I sold radio advertising for years, and they say frequency matters, especially when you are bombarded with millions of messages each day. Our consumption of content is off the charts now with social media. I really don't know how our brains can handle the influx, and I can't even begin to fathom what it will be like in the next thirty years. I just know that thirty years ago these four elements worked, and maybe thirty years from now they will continue to keep working for people. Maybe Siri and Alexa and whatever AI at the time will be able to pull together the wisdom of your network and refine it to exactly what you Need and are looking for rather than the overload we get. As we grow Needworking, maybe it's something we can help with.

Digital advertising has been personalizing advertising to you for years. I worked at Advertising.com, which specialized in targeting audiences based on third-party cookies and data. At the time of writing, Google is eliminating third-party cookies and switching to non-identifying Topics. The concept of Needworking is focusing on your top-level Topics.

The Needworking platform will not have spammy content to get you to click; there are already more social platforms than we Need, and it's overload. We want to make sure you are building your own professional network and focusing on the important things that will help build or maintain your career and professional goals to shift your Networking into G.E.A.R.:

- → Groups
- → Events
- → Allies
- → Reciprocity/Referrals

That's it, really. It comes down to not overwhelming yourself and not continuously trying to overload social media with loads of content and trying to compete with all the social creators.

I would add that relevant content like articles/Needworking Insights and emails are great for helping someone's knowledge base. If you want to build deeper relationships with people you can do business with, this is as simple as it gets.

Now, you probably have an opinion on this, and you might disagree with me. You might think it's a lot bigger than this and that I don't understand your world and what you Need to accomplish, and this will never fit into what you are trying to do.

You're right. You are on your own journey, and content is king. Maybe it's your thing, and you're good at producing videos. You will have a lot more on your plate, as most people do. If it works for you, do it.

If that's the case, you are already creating your own groups. You have built a fan base that feels you are an ally, you may have created a fan event, and you might have asked your followers for their opinion at some point and they responded.

I know you don't have to follow this methodology, because everyone has their own formula for success. I am just sharing with you what I've learned during the years of experience growing a network of awesome individuals who have supported all my crazy ideas, and I am truly grateful for them. I'll go deeper into the Ally building later, but I wouldn't be here today if it weren't for Allies.

This writing comes about a year after we launched the beta of Needworking, and if it wasn't for those who continue to come back and participate, this book wouldn't exist. I have had the Core 4 in my head as the original full buildout, but we had to gradually build the platform over time and build it publicly to get feedback.

Networking is all about engaging. How you engage is up to you, but by utilizing the Core 4 elements, you should see success every time you refine your skills.

The Intersection of Maslow's Needs and Networking

The Hierarchy of Networking

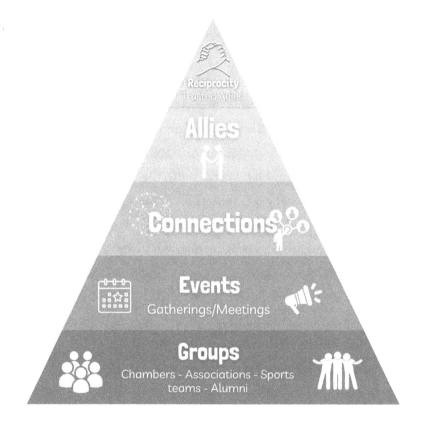

The intersection of Maslow's Hierarchy of Needs and the envisioned Networking Hierarchy presents a compelling perspective on the alignment between fundamental human Needs and the dynamics of forming professional connections.

At the foundational level, there's the Need for belonging, social interaction, and safety. Maslow's Love and Belonging Need is akin to the initial layer of Groups, Associations, and Chambers of Commerce in the Networking Hierarchy. These entities establish a sense of belonging and a secure environment for individuals to embark on their networking journey.

Progressing upwards, Maslow's Safety Need aligns with the Networking Hierarchy's subsequent level of Events. These events create opportunities for common engagement, shared experiences, and the fostering of safety through collective interaction.

Ascending further, we encounter the Esteem Need in Maslow's model, which parallels the Networking Hierarchy's concept of making Connections. Establishing professional relationships involves gaining recognition and respect within specific circles, contributing to one's sense of esteem and self-worth.

At the Self-Actualization stage in Maslow's framework, individuals seek personal growth and the realization of their potential. This corresponds to the Networking Hierarchy's Allies level. Allies represent like-minded individuals pursuing mutual goals, propelling each other towards greater achievements through collaboration.

The upper tiers of both hierarchies—Trusted Allies in Networking and Self-Actualization in Maslow's model—signify the culmination of human development and networking efforts. The synergy is evident: just as self-actualization entails reaching the pinnacle of one's potential, Trusted Allies signify relationships built on profound trust and shared objectives. These Allies mutually contribute to each other's aspirations.

The envisioned Reciprocity, akin to Maslow's Self-Transcendence concept, forms the apex of the combined hierarchy. Reciprocity entails giving back, creating a symbiotic networking relationship where both parties benefit. This reflects the fulfillment of one's networking journey while concurrently contributing to the growth and success of others.

In summary, the fusion of Maslow's Hierarchy of Needs with the envisioned Networking Hierarchy showcases how core human Needs for belonging, safety, recognition, growth, and self-transcendence align with the progressive stages of cultivating professional relationships. It underscores how addressing these Needs through strategic networking leads to a comprehensive sense of achievement and interconnected success.

The Takeaway

Building a powerful network goes beyond overwhelming yourself with excessive content or random social media interactions. Instead, it revolves around focusing on your topic of expertise and understanding how others can benefit from it. By following the four core principles of G.E.A.R.— Groups, Events, Allies, and Reciprocity—you can strategically build a network that aligns with your career and provides value to others:

1. **Groups:** Join and actively participate in groups that are relevant to your current career goals. These groups can serve as valuable platforms to connect with like-minded professionals, exchange knowledge, and expand your network. Remember, you can always reassess and switch groups as your journey evolves.

2. **Events:** Invest your time wisely by attending events that are directly related to your topic of expertise. By

immersing yourself in the right environments, you increase your chances of connecting with individuals who share similar interests and can contribute to your professional growth.

3. **Allies:** Choose your Allies thoughtfully, seeking individuals who align with your values and goals. Focus on cultivating meaningful relationships with these like-minded individuals who can provide support, guidance, and potential collaborations. Building a network of Allies fosters a mutually beneficial environment for growth and opportunity.

4. **Reciprocity/Referrals:** Actively engage in conversations where you can offer valuable advice and assistance within your area of expertise. By positioning yourself as a reliable resource and actively helping others, you not only gain gratitude from those you assist but also showcase your expertise to a wider audience.

By implementing these core principles, you can build a network centered around your topic of expertise. This approach allows you to provide value to others while establishing yourself as a trusted and reliable professional in your field. Remember, networking is not just about making connections; it's about leveraging your expertise to create meaningful and mutually beneficial relationships.

CHAPTER 6

GROUPS AND COMMUNITIES

S o let's take a little journey back to your childhood and where it all began. Take some time to think about the groups or communities you belonged to. Did you join a rec league for sports? Do you recall anyone who was in the league? Were you a part of a Girl, Cub, or Boy Scout troop, maybe 4-H? I'm sure you have memories, whether good or bad, of those events. I have lots of memories of belonging or not belonging stored in my memory banks, as do most people. I recall when I felt left out of my Scout group. That was the night in 1978 when NBC was premiering *KISS Meets the Phantom of the Park*. Every kid was talking about going home and watching it. I was so excited to turn on the TV and talk about it with them the next day at school.

The only problem that I hadn't counted on was my parents. They weren't about to let me watch anything that was centered around a rock group that had fake blood dripping out of their mouths and played over-the-top rock. Their speed was Frank Sinatra, Barry Manilow, and Glen Campbell, and they hadn't acquired a taste for music that was from Woodstock or beyond, so KISS was definitely out of the question. Come to think of it, I still haven't seen that movie; maybe it's time.

In that moment of time, I felt left out and alone. We have all certainly been on a journey, and we all have felt left out and alone. How many years have passed since you last thought of those connections or moments? Where are they now? I have spoken to so many people who have felt the same way, that they didn't find their tribe until college, their work environment, or even their new neighborhood. You might be connected to those whom you knew from high school, but are they close Allies? One of my closest friends still to this day, Joe, is from elementary school, and he is in my circle of Trusted Allies, and you can find him Needworking with others.

I know you have met thousands of people, maybe tens of thousands in your lifetime. What brings them into your group of trusted connections? Have you taken the time and actually researched your Facebook friends from high school or college? What are they doing now, and how can that relate to what you're trying to achieve?

Let's just use me as an example now. If we are talking about growing a group or community, I'm the perfect study. I'm trying to build a networking community for everyone else. It's not just a community, but more of a community with processes of what I believe networking should look like. For me personally, I can tell you it's been difficult to bring my Facebook and LinkedIn connections over to Needworking.

I can't put my finger on why. I start to doubt myself when people I've known for decades don't join in what I'm doing, and there's so many feelings that go along with that. First off, coming from a kid who was given up at birth, there's a whole slew of abandonment issues going on. Then there's the wins. When someone does jump onto Needworking to try it, it gives you something to hold on to. A sort of "maybe I'm not so crazy after all" moment. But then that person might not post anything on Needworking after that, and it all starts over again, the self-doubt and longing for people to join. You wonder why they didn't support you, especially when you know you have supported them in the past. Maybe you are just overthinking the whole thing, and people are busy with their own lives and own agendas. Maybe some don't even like to be on social media.

Organizing and growing your own groups is difficult, especially when humans are pulled in so many directions. The great thing is you have a choice. Create your group or join one that is already created, and move forward with the mindset you share.

The important thing is that you, just like me, want to belong to something more meaningful. I had the opportunity to see Priya Parker open SXSW in 2022, and she spoke about her book, *The Art of Gathering*. She talked about being the host of the gathering and the things a host does to engage and connect the room.

1. Why we are all coming together; what's the NEED?
2. The introductions and connecting guests to one another.
3. The host protects their guests from one another with rules for the group.
4. They equalize the room and connect them with context.

I'm sure you already know what happened next. Yes, I walked up to the front of the stage and introduced myself and introduced Needworking to her. What's the worst thing that could happen? Nothing, and that's where that has led so far. I'm hopeful that one day we will have her as a part of the Needworking platform and can provide some detailed gathering information for users. We were pushed away for the next speaker and I never had a chance to ask for a meeting.

You've probably already noticed by now: I believe in the Law of Attraction. I believe in putting your Needs out to the universe, Especially to your Allies and connections. You'll never know what you'll get back unless you ask.

So how do you find groups and organizations that make sense for you? Where do you start, especially if you are new to an organization, an area, or just getting started in your career? The first thing to be clear on is whom are you trying to connect with? Is it a local neighborhood association, is it business networking, or is it that Big Rock (large client) that you want to go after?

Let's start with some simple things like Meetup.com or Event-brite. You can do a quick search there and look for a subject to see if anything might be happening that is in your area of interest. You should take the time to look and see if it's worthwhile.

Ask people you are already connected to. Professionals looking for opportunities to connect have probably been involved in several organized communities. I have created a list of organizations that have been using Needworking for event postings and for group communications in the reference section.

Now, we have discussed events previously, and I know this might be redundant, but the reality is that you should search again to see if you may have missed something, and you never know who is hosting the event. It's not so much the event I want you to focus on, but the organizer. I just did a search for networking on Meetup and found a lot of BNI groups posting events.

I am a fan of Dr. Ivan Misner, the founder of BNI, author of many books, and a master of networking and referral-based gatherings. I mentioned him in the introduction. I enjoyed meeting new people at my local BNI meetings, but the time commitment was always a deterrent for me. If you are comfortable with trading leads and connections, this might be a good place to start. I have spoken to many networkers who are reluctant to follow the BNI model of providing referrals that include their contact's information. If these are Trusted Allies of yours, would you be breaking their trust or relationship by sharing their contact information with someone else?

Some swear by the BNI program, and what is right for you is what you are most comfortable with, so don't worry about what others say. Our philosophies and principles of Needworking are aligned with some of Misner's work and writings. I would recommend reading his networking strategies and beliefs if you're interested in a deeper dive into networking.

I personally like the way Ivan Misner and Brian Hilliard break out groups in their book *Networking like a Pro*:

1. **Casual contact networks** — Regularly meet with social events and mixers monthly, and you have to exert the effort to connect and get the referral (Chambers, Alumni, Speaker Series).
2. **Strong contact networks** — Meet weekly, members must exchange referrals, and membership is limited to specific people or categories in the room (BNI, Pacesetters).
3. **Community service clubs** — Nonprofits or civic duties that bring communities together for good.
4. **Professional associations** — Usually a paid membership in specialty organizations bringing similar professionals together (such as construction, tourism, health, architects). The purpose is to exchange ideas and information.

5. **Online/social media networks** — I don't think I Need to explain this one!

The key to finding good groups is looking for the right fit. Find people who you feel will help you build a lasting relationship and, most importantly, let you know how you can help the group. I can honestly say I stretch myself too thin trying to get to different events. Running between multiple markets for in-person events is a grind. I attend events in multiple cities, and it isn't easy. Staying in one locale or concentrating on your topic of expertise is key to having a strong network.

How to Find a Good Group

Let's look at some ways to find a group. You might be interested in groups based on locality, whether they are faith-based or not, part of the same alumni group as you, or whether they are chambers of commerce or business groups. There are also sports-oriented social groups and associations. Let's look more closely at each one.

Locality

You may choose groups that allow you to stay close to home if you live in an area where you can manage a territory and be an active participant. They say the key to real estate investment is location, location, location. That's true with networking as well. Invest in yourself and find the location you want to be in. It's difficult to transition to a new location and build relationships, so you have to be committed and in it for the long haul. If you plan on not investing your time and effort, people see and sense that, and you will be excluded.

I personally would not recommend getting involved with groups that are more than forty five-to-sixty miles apart unless you can manage your accounts/business and your whole goal is just getting facetime. You have to be invested not only in the group but also in the community. Depending on your career, this is a variable. Architects and musicians can go further distances, especially if they are in a niche that no one else offers locally. If you are a mortgage broker, HVAC seller, restaurant, or insurance broker, there is enough business in your backyard to focus your time and effort on your community.

I would first look at the Designated Market Area (DMA) you are in. Nielsen built these lists years ago for television and radio, and media platforms like Facebook and Google have adopted them into their advertising models.

Some markets are close together and you can get away with coverage in multiple areas. Since I'm from Baltimore, I can use this as an example. If you live north of Baltimore City closer to Pennsylvania, it doesn't make sense to network in Washington, DC. You talk different sport teams and don't randomly bump into people you know.

As an example, I had a quickie lunch recently with someone I used to work with and was trying to get a referral to help propel our businesses. We walked out of the restaurant and bumped into two people he knew through his daughters' school. I attended the same college as both of them, and they have been in my circle of connections for years. It gives me a reason to reach back out now, because it was a limited window of what I call the "Hi and Bye Opportunity." In other words, just say hello and don't spew your sales jargon at that moment; instead recall, research, and reconnect.

Now that same interaction probably wouldn't happen for me in DC because I'm not there as often. Unless I'm at a targeted event/ group meeting, it's less likely,

Being in the same location and area is key to random networking. Don't just sit at home all day if your job is getting out there. If you have to do online work, go sit in a local coffee shop and get noticed. Don't do this every day but maybe once a week on different days. You want the casual uniqueness of being seen even if it was intentional. You have to find a key location where people linger, perhaps not necessarily the local Starbucks, since people tend to order on the app and roll out.

In Baltimore, I like to visit the Stone Mill Bakery, Baltimore Coffee and Tea, and many more. I met with Amina Weiskerger, the then-executive director of an awesome nonprofit called ShareBaby, which provides Maryland babies and children living in shelters ages zero to five with basic items such as clothing, diapers, toys, and equipment. She suggested a place called The Corner Pantry. I had never been, and I had driven by it a million times since my old company was practically right next door. She was like the mayor of that establishment and knew everyone because it was her neighborhood of professionals, parents with kids in school, and synagogue-goers. When you find a gem like that, use the "Hi and Bye" method to your advantage.

Now in some markets you can get away with working two regions; if you live in the lower part of Maryland closer to DC, it makes sense to call DC home base and travel to specific Baltimore events. Smaller markets' DMAs are typically excited to get participation from bigger DMAs.

Philadelphia and Wilmington are tightly connected, and you can do this joint market when one market has dominance over the other.

It's extremely difficult working DMAs of the same size like Richmond/ Baltimore/Pittsburgh; not only are they too far away from each other, but you'll never get the traction you Need to be successful. New York and Philadelphia are relatively close by train, and yet you still have the same issues: different sports teams, different schools and communities, and fewer ways to connect.

If you aren't building a large-scale community networking project like ours, stay in your area and be the pillar of your community. Use social connector tools like Facebook and Nextdoor.

In her book *Own Your Network*, Nadia Bilchik brings up some great examples of location-based events that correlate with your career and community. She states, "Venues that relate to your professional interests are particularly valuable. For example, a Georgia-based-journalist could go to Atlanta Press Club events." The National Press Club in Washington, DC, is also a big central point for networking, just like the Atlanta Press Club. The National Press Club is a professional and social club for working journalists and communications professionals that has been a Washington institution for more than a century.

The benefit of joining a club like this is that not only do you get access to their club and meeting their members, but you can connect with others at reciprocal clubs. Let's say you become a member of Baltimore's Center Club. This will give you access to ninety-two other clubs in the US and internationally. This includes clubs like the St. James Club in Paris, The Union League in Philadelphia, The Sloane Club in London, and The National Press Club.

One of the last features we added to Needworking.com was spaces. Groups are always looking for accommodating locations to meet. So if you know of someone with a fun networking space in your area, tell them to add it to the platform.

Faith-Based Communities

There is something to be said about how people of faith can help others in their time of Need. One of the activities most overlooked in terms of networking potential is getting together with members of your local church, mosque, synagogue, or wherever you practice religion. People come together when they have common values and can raise communities. There is nothing more rewarding than being a part of a group that is helping, learning, sharing, and caring about one another.

How much time are you spending in the faith-based world? Depression increases and health declines when you aren't connecting and providing positive life experiences to one another.

There are many business networking groups that connect around faith. You can do a simple search on Google and find a faith-based business networking group, or call your local faith gathering place and ask.

Alumni (High School, College, Cohorts, Fraternity, Sorority)

How often do you reach out to your college or high school alumni group for support? The answer probably is not often enough. LinkedIn is a great resource to dive back down into a network where you already have something in common with other members: your alma mater's alumni network. If you take the time to do research, you will find potential connections and opportunities you may have not thought of.

If you have done any business accelerator courses or certification classes, take some time each week to reengage with someone in your class who you feel might be a relevant connection to what you are trying to accomplish.

As much as I grieve about the clutter in LinkedIn feeds, there is no better way to connect with someone from your university. As of this writing there are universities with alumni networks on LinkedIn that equal the populations of small cities. Here's a sample:

- Clemson: 138,000
- University of Maryland: 335,000
- University of Michigan: 345,000
- University of Oklahoma: 170,000
- Florida State: 250,000

That's a pretty big pool of prospects and connections and maybe a great place to spend your research time. If you attended one of these colleges or universities, you already have something in common with others in that network. That list is only going to increase the older you get.

The great thing about LinkedIn and the data they have gathered over the years is that you can see where the alumni work, what they do, where they live. It's the perfect place to research and reach out to potential new Allies to help grow your business.

Recently I have become more engaged with my alma mater, Towson University (Towson State when I went there). They have over 120,000 alumni engaged on LinkedIn, and a friend of mine heads up the Towson University Business Alumni Association (TUBLA). One of the first events I attended was a few years ago, and it shocked me to see people in the room whom I already did business with and didn't realize we had gone to the same college. It provided a tighter connection for us and a more definitive way for us to do business together based on that deeper connection. Had I done my research in advance, I would have looked at my first-level connections on LinkedIn that had gone to the university.

I also recommend you stay connected with your Allies that you had in business class or business training. See what they are up to, and ask for references.

Chambers of Commerce and Business Networking Groups

Local chambers are great for the locality of doing business in areas where you live or spend most of your time. It's the closest thing to your home base to make connections, and you can join multiple chambers or business networking groups to expand your reach. Again, just don't spread yourself too thin.

An article on the US Chamber website (https://www.uschamber. com/co/start/strategy/experts-explain-how-to-network) offers tips on how to network at chamber meetings. The first tip is to focus on giving and listening. Imagine that; where have you heard that before? Frequency is key, so if we all agree that helping and giving is the best way to connect, this world will be a much better place.

Chambers are a mix of every type of business you can find. If you were to take a member snapshot of a chamber in Sacramento and a chamber in Schenectady (which, by the way, is a huge chamber in upstate New York called the Capital Region Chamber), you'll find very similar member companies and dynamics.

If you feel you aren't the chamber type, there are a tremendous number of business networking and corridor associations that may be the right fit. The key to these connections and groups is that they are providing you with helpful connections and you follow through on them.

Sports Social Groups

Sports social groups are a great way to connect and stay healthy. I used to be a part of our radio station's softball teams, and we had a media league where we would play other radio and TV stations. Media outlets are extremely competitive.

You might have played in a league yourself, and the person who plays the position right next to you could be your next biggest client. Don't just have conversations about sports and your home teams. Ask about business and ask if there is anyone in their organization that you can meet with to discuss what you have to offer. You won't be putting them in a bad position unless they aren't in a good position at the job they are currently doing. YOU STILL HAVE TO ASK!

Mastermind Groups

Mastermind groups offer a distinctive fusion of collaborative brainstorming, peer accountability, and mutual support, refining both business and personal skills. The combined efforts of a mastermind group contribute to the individual success of its members, cultivating an environment where challenges are met, ambitious goals are set, and most importantly, achieved.

Functioning as a wealth of creative ideas and supportive decision-making, the group transforms into a forum for sharing triumphs and navigating challenges as success plans are implemented.

Celebrating successes with enthusiasm and collectively addressing problems through innovative thinking, the group serves as a secure space for like-minded individuals. Discussions within the group can span business owner issues or delve into vulnerable, personal matters.

Active involvement in the group necessitates commitment, confidentiality, and a willingness to give and receive advice and ideas. Members offer unwavering support marked by honesty, respect, and compassion. In the mastermind group, participants embody roles such as growth catalysts, devil's advocates, and supportive colleagues, encapsulating the essence and value of these groups.

I am part of a highly supportive group of nine individuals that convenes monthly. Our paths have intertwined over the years in various capacities, and we have united to hold ourselves accountable and establish a robust support system. Our three-hour meetings serve as an excellent sounding board and a rich knowledge base. Some members also participate in other regional mastermind groups like INSIGHT ConneX and Vistage, which may host monthly or weekly meetings, as well as large quarterly events. These larger events, while more akin to networking, differ from the focused nature of smaller mastermind groups. If you explore online, you are likely to discover several mastermind groups in your area that could provide significant value.

Military Camaraderie

In the military, it's all about having each other's backs, and that starts with building tight-knit crews during training. When you're sweating it out together, facing insane challenges, you bond in a way that's hard to explain. It's like you become family, relying on each other through the toughest of times. You learn to trust your buddies with your life because, hey, you've seen them push through the same stuff you have.

And when it's game time out there, those bonds are everything. In the heat of battle, you gotta know the person next to you has got your six. It's not just about following orders; it's about knowing your team inside and out, understanding how they move and think. Plus, it's not just your unit; it's the whole military community. When you build allies, you're not just building connections, you're building a support system that runs deep, from the top brass down to the newest recruit.

Associations

I'm saving the best for last, and that is centering around the Needworking platform's Topics again. Associations are one of the best resources for a person to get involved with. The key is to know your customer personas. A persona represents an imagined, representative character specifically designed to cater to the users or customers of your business. It personifies the ideal individual for your business to serve, embodying the precise challenges your product addresses, the objectives it helps accomplish, and possessing sensibilities that resonate and establish a connection with your brand. There is a huge correlation between the events and groups you belong to. Stay connected in those circles if they are a key type of client or industry topic for what you are trying to accomplish.

If you are looking to get into that industry, you can find a way to make connections and find opportunities and people that can help.

Back when I was working at a small web design company, I wanted to be a part of a big internet company. We had six employees where I worked, and I was cutting my teeth on learning SEO and paid search in 2004 and wanted to find a large company where I could share my expertise as well as learn more.

The problem was I lived in Baltimore and I had two young children, and I couldn't leave the area because the kids were here and my wife at the time didn't want to move to New York or California. Maryland wasn't known for accommodating tech giants.

I was a part of the local Advertising Associations, and I wondered what the New York-based associations had to offer me. The Advertising Club of New York (https://www.theadvertisingclub.org/) was my answer on how to break into the large companies. I had been going to national events like Search Engine Strategies and meeting the companies, but many of them were based in California.

The Ad Club was trying to generate more funding, so they listed their holiday party and all of the auction items online. One of the auction items was breakfast with Wenda Harris Millard, and I was determined to win that auction item. Wenda was the chief sales officer at Yahoo! at the time and larger than life to me. She drove billions of advertising dollars to Yahoo!, and her team came up with groundbreaking internet ad experiences. For me, the problem with this auction was that it wasn't an online auction but in person at their holiday party in New York City. I had to get a ticket, take a train up, win the auction, and get back at a reasonable hour because my ex would have never gone for it. I said I was determined, and I did it. I walked around that table and watched those bids like a hawk. I felt there was no way I would go through all of this trouble just to go home empty-handed.

Needless to say, Wenda and I did have breakfast, and I felt like a stranger in a strange land. The advertising dollars for Yahoo and Google and her New York connections were so far apart from the realm of the reality that I lived in. The whole experience was incredible. Wenda invited me to an awards ceremony after the breakfast (she's won so many awards). I even got to sit next to her close friend cheering her on, Martha Stewart (you may have heard of her).

Although NYC wasn't an option for me, shortly after that I got the job at Advertising.com and was part of AOL after they were acquired. The beauty of it all was they were headquartered in Baltimore, and I didn't have to be away from my kids. So stay focused on your topic, be relentless and determined, and good things will happen.

The Takeaway

This chapter has explored the importance of belonging to groups and communities and how they can positively impact our lives. I've shared the challenges I've faced in building my own networking community and the importance of finding the right fit for personal and professional growth.

Connect with like-minded individuals, because the benefits of being part of groups aligned with your interests and goals are crucial. You can find and join groups by utilizing online platforms like Meetup.com and Eventbrite, attending events, and exploring professional associations. Consider locality and community involvement as key factors when choosing groups to join.

Faith-based communities offer us an often overlooked potential for networking and supporting one another.

Find meaningful groups and communities to enhance your personal and professional growth, and invest time and effort in building relationships within your community. Seek out opportunities for connection and collaboration.

CHAPTER 7

NEEDWORKING AT EVENTS— BUILD YOUR NETWORK OF ALLIES

I f you are new to the networking scene it can be very intimidating, especially walking into a room where everyone already knows each other. After dealing with Covid-19 and lockdowns in 2020 and 2021, people are getting back together at a furious pace. You have to pick and choose your events carefully now to make sure you get the right benefit and create your own ways of efficient networking.

I've been going to networking events for decades, and I have my own style of walking up to people and joining a conversation. Sometimes I get to a point at going to these events where I just talk to the staff working them because I was in the service industry, and sometimes it's intimidating to connect with others in the room. I try to research a specific topic in advance of going to a specialized conference where I might not be familiar with the subject matter or persons in attendance.

If you are looking for tips on networking styles and improving your networking, you could read a book like *Networking for People Who Hate Networking* by Devora Zack. The subtitle is *A Field Guide For Introverts, The Overwhelmed, and The Underconnected.* In addition to tips, there are workbook sections that will help the novice and even those who Need a refresher course in connecting.

For the purpose of this book, let's discuss how the Needworking platform intersects with in-person networking, focusing both on the networker (Needworker) and the group or event planner in this chapter.

Creating, organizing, and even attending meetings can sometimes be extremely draining for organizers and their participants. Some people just aren't great at meeting other people at networking events, either in person or online. There are so many reasons that we can't begin to imagine what is happening with each individual. Our goal is to help create meetings and interactions that are fun and uplifting, and not uncomfortable or like it's a waste of time. The concept behind Needworking is that we want to accomplish three things:

1. **Connect with an Ally who can help you fulfill your Needs.** If they can't help you personally, they can help you find the answer or connect you with a person who can.

2. **"Speed Networking," breakfast meetings, and happy hours don't usually let you share enough of your story to connect with someone.** You Need to slow the process down and present what is important to you and why. Tell your story to as many people as will listen. Speed is not the answer; diving deeper and learning about a company is.

3. **Presenting a Need and getting more specific will cut down on the time you have wasted just chit-chatting and not accomplishing your goal.** People can help you get to the next level, and in turn, you should reciprocate by giving that help to others.

4. **Make sure the event you are attending is the right event for you.** Are these the people you should be connecting with? Are they in the right target group for what you are trying to accomplish?

A Guide to Using Needworking

Here's a simple guide on how to use Needworking.com and the Needworking processes within your event planning and structuring organized Networking.

1) Connect with the Right People to Build Your Allies

If you haven't yet identified who that customer is, what's stopping you? Get an idea of who the right fit is and narrow your focus to connecting with them. Recently we bought a booth at a local trade show, and we knew we were spinning our wheels because it wasn't the right audience. However, the reason I did this was because I was targeting one person out of the 5,000 people in attendance. As I was hoping, he stopped by the booth, and we are doing business with him now. I wouldn't necessarily recommend that be your approach, but we did get some other meetings set up, and it was a nice added bonus.

Depending on your product, you Need to put together your typical customer persona. You know those avatars you create for your profile pictures and bitmoji? Yes, build those based on questions that might surround who your ideal customer match is. Look at all of your current customers and who they keep company with, and build out what we in digital marketing call look-alike audiences. They have a higher probability of doing business with you because of their demographic or psychographic profile.

If you already have an existing customer base, you can ask them directly why they do business with you or if they would refer you to other businesses.

Here are a few questions that might help you creating your customer profiles/personas:

➜ What size company are they?
➜ What is their annual revenue?
➜ Which events do they or their employees typically attend?
➜ What's their job title?
➜ What are their goals?
➜ What are their values?
➜ What are their interests?
➜ What challenges do they face?
➜ What are their pain points?
➜ Where do they get their news?
➜ Which social media platforms do they use?
➜ What sports do they watch or participate in?
➜ How do they decide to spend their money?
➜ Who makes the decision to spend that money?

I know that not all of the above questions may be relevant to your business or product, but you can add others and take away what you feel is not appropriate. These questions are meant to be guidelines. The reality is that you Need to put yourself in your customers' shoes and create a detailed profile that would be the ideal customer to reach out to regularly. If they don't match with the people at these events you are attending, what is your next plan?

You can interview previous and current customers directly or send out surveys to learn more about them.

HubSpot has done a lot of work helping businesses define buyer personas. I would recommend using the buyer persona tool on their website to help you in figuring out yours; see https://blog.hubspot.com/marketing/buyer-persona-research.

You can also do a search on Needworking to find people who are interested in specific Topics:

2) Be Unique and Stand Out

One of the things I've been doing lately is basically wearing a uniform at these events. Most men are in blazers and button-down or polo shirts; not me. I've been wearing a green long sleeve Needworking shirt, with big lettering on the front that you can't miss. On the back of the shirt is a QR code for people to scan to get to the Needworking website. For my QR codes, I personally like 1stPartyQR.com. There are plenty of free QR Code software tools you can utilize to get attention and retarget traffic back to your brand. I know it's not the sexiest or most professional thing to do, but sometimes I'll wear a sport coat on top to give it a dressier look. Right now I just want to spread the word about Needworking, especially if I'm at a networking event…and it works. People see my shirt from across the room, and they have to ask what we do. I also get some scans here and there.

Another benefit are the group pictures or the random photos I find myself in. It definitely helps me stand out in the crowd of everyone who is at a given networking event. I've also used the tactic at events where I knew absolutely no one, and it helped break the ice, because people are so curious.

Yes, it might be a little hokey, but people expect me to wear it now, and they are at the point of wondering why I'm not wearing the brand if I show up wearing something other than this green shirt. I'm quite proud of the Needworking name and brand; the "ki" in

"Needworking" is two people meeting and shaking hands. You have to be unique at times to get noticed. There's a gentleman in Baltimore who walks around at every festival, in bars, and at events who has his picture taken and posted on dozens of Instagram accounts. He is known for his signature bow tie, rimmed glasses, and top hat. We all know him as Bow Tie Bob, and he has become something of a legend and celebrity in town. Bob is probably in his upper sixties or seventies and is having the time of his life out and about. I'm not suggesting you use these tactics if it's not your style, but the key is figuring out how to stand out in a crowded space where everyone has a different Need.

Jim Ries, who recently interviewed me for his "Java with Jim" vlog (video blog), has a signature cap he wears, not out at events but as part of his online persona: a spiky, furry cap. People recognize it, and locally, everyone knows Jim because he is a Superconnector. Feel free to connect with him on Needworking; he could become one of your trusted and true Allies. It just takes time to build that trust with the likes of Jim.

If you are uncomfortable going to events, grab a friend (an ally) and team up to divide and conquer. Try to meet different people in different parts of the room. If you are part of a small sales group, break the room up but don't try to get business cards from as many people as you can; that is Needy and desperate. Going back to what we covered in the previous chapter, you want to make that meet-and-greet time valuable and dive a little deeper with people. I was at a Baltimore Tourism Association meeting and discovered that members will go out to events, gather business cards as a group. They trade and share them in follow up discussions; they are not just out to further themselves. They help bring business and connections back for the betterment of the organization.

3) *Tell Your Story to as Many People As Will Listen*

When I worked in radio, I had a boss, Alan Leinwand, who created a list of "Rules to Live By" for the sales team. One of Alan's rules was "tell all who will listen". He was proud of that list, and I'm sure he took it to every company he worked for. To be honest, it was a good list for someone young in the industry. It brought a little structure into the craziness of selling radio ads and competing with local radio stations, television stations, newspapers, magazines, and direct mail in the days before the internet came into the mix. I can only imagine what it's like now. If you have ever seen the street fights in the films *Anchorman* or *Anchorman 2,* it's reminiscent of stations just coming out of nowhere scrapping for advertisers' money. It was quite a scene back in the day, especially if you didn't get on an availed buy (money allocated on behalf of the advertiser).

I agree with the idea of telling all who will listen in principle, because you have to find many ears, but you also have to find the right audience. If your story doesn't resonate with the group you've connected with, it's a waste of time. If there was anything I could change about Leinwand's rule, it would be to add that, as well as stressing the importance of listening back. It's more important to engage with your audience than it is to throw up your sales or elevator pitch all over them.

Connect with them and listen to what they have to say. Then tell your story and how it relates to them and how it can help their business or provide a stronger reason to connect.

The summer of 2022 I went around to bars and restaurants in Ocean City, Maryland, and handed out green and white Needworking pens to the waitresses and owners. I was known as the pen guy. I would get random calls from people I knew saying they signed their check with a Needworking pen. The following summer we were at a popular restaurant/bar in Ocean City, Seacrets. As we were ordering we noticed that green and white Needworking pen in the pocket of the waitress. It again led to an opportunity to tell the story about why she had that pen and what Needworking is.

> "I've learned that people will forget what you said, people will forget what you did, but people will never forget how you made them feel."
>
> **MAYA ANGELOU,**
> **POET AND CIVIL RIGHTS ACTIVIST**

4) Present Your Need in Advance

Networking is hard, and knowing how to work a room can be difficult. When you post on social media that you are planning to attend an event, tell people why you are going and whom you would like to connect with.

Besides just asking for what you Need, maybe tell others how you can help them in your social profiles, including Needworking. It's what our platform was meant for. Superheroes show up in the nick of time to help others in Need. What is your superpower? How can you help others in Need? I'm a huge comics geek and have thousands of comics and can't wait for the release of new superhero TV shows or movies. It's actually not a bad idea to add a question like that on our platform. Asking "Who's your favorite superhero" might be a fun idea. It's a great talking point, and most people can relate to a hero.

I would say post how you can help others on your social profile. You can also comment and let them know in advance that you will be attending an event, and share how you might be able to support others. If you are just telling people that you want to connect over insurance benefits for a business or that you specialize in leaf guard protectors, you have a lot of competition. Get ready for your own street fight. If you can tell your audience what sets you apart, then you can truly build your Justice League, Avengers, Defenders, or Suicide Squad. No matter what super networking team you build, your audience/network Needs to know how you can help them.

If you Need a refresher course or just don't know how to create that brand of yours or don't understand what your superpower is, then you Need to do a deep dive with yourself and figure it out. I would recommend *Book Yourself Solid* by Michael Port. I randomly downloaded the audio book because my calendar was a little light. At first I thought, I don't Need this. I've been in business for how many years, and I can set meetings all day long. I'm glad I didn't listen to that inner voice and took the time to listen to his book. He also has a great workbook you can download as well; see https://ldryanconlon.com/wp-content/uploads/2020/05/BookYourselfSolid-Lead-Generation-Workbook.pdf.

Port takes you through processes of creating your brand and getting down to what problem you are solving for people. That's your superpower. As he puts it, "A personal brand is a combination of who you are, what you do and why you do it. Your personal brand is based on which problems you solve for whom, why people should come to you, and what results your solutions produce. In order to find out your personal brand, ask yourself questions such as: What makes me different or even eccentric?"

As an example, I made the fatal mistake of telling people my company Enradius is a digital marketing company that specializes in geotargeting. Blah blah blah. I keep forgetting that I'm still in an actual street fight because there are thousands of businesses that exist that can say they do the same thing. With all the companies out there generalizing, you feel more like a sidekick.

So I decided to flip the switch on that and say, "Enradius specializes in the customer journey, discovering where people are coming from before they reach your front door and where they are going after they leave." Wow, it's like I have X-ray vision now!

With the first description of my company, people don't react, and they don't ask questions. It's an "is what it is" kind of statement. In the improved version, people want to know how it's done, and they want to see an example, because now they are curious. Yes, tell your story to all that will listen, but make sure the story isn't the same story that everyone else is telling. Set yourself apart.

The Takeaway

1. Choose your networking events wisely: With the resurgence of in-person events, it's important to be selective and attend gatherings that align with your goals. Focus on events where you can find the right connections and make meaningful progress.

2. Utilize the Needworking platform: Learn how the Needworking platform intersects with in-person networking. Understand how it benefits both the networker (Needworker) and the event planner, and leverage its features to enhance your networking efforts.

3. Connect with the right people: Identify your target audience and create customer profiles or personas. Understand their characteristics, interests, and challenges to connect more effectively. Use resources like HubSpot's buyer persona tool to assist you in defining your ideal customer.

4. Stand out from the crowd: Find unique ways to differentiate yourself at events. Consider wearing distinctive attire or accessories that spark curiosity and initiate conversations. Be memorable and make a lasting impression.

5. Engage and listen: When telling your story, focus on engaging with your audience and understanding their Needs. Actively listen to their perspectives and tailor your message to resonate with them. Remember Maya Angelou's quote: "People will never forget how you made them feel."

6. Present your Needs in advance: When attending events, share your intentions and desired connections on social media or other platforms. Also, highlight how you can help others, emphasizing your unique value proposition. Be ready to contribute and support others as well.

7. Define your brand and superpower: Take the time to identify your personal brand and understand the specific problems you solve for your target audience. Communicate your value in a compelling and differentiated way. Consider resources like *Book Yourself Solid* by Michael Port to refine your brand and offerings.

In summary, effective networking requires strategic event selection, leveraging Needworking, connecting with the right people, standing out, engaging authentically, presenting your Needs, and developing a clear personal brand. By implementing these strategies, you can build a network of Allies and achieve your networking goals.

> "The person who follows the crowd will usually go no further than the crowd. The person who walks alone is likely to find himself in places no one has ever seen before."
>
> **– ALBERT EINSTEIN**

CHAPTER 8

ATTEND THE RIGHT EVENTS AND START THE CONVERSATION

I have attended thousands of events, but I know that connections can be made anywhere. Pamela, one of our sales reps, randomly met a future client while in line for lunch. You don't have to have a planned event to make a good connection, but it helps.

There are so many different events that you could spend the majority of your time going from one event to the next, and it can lead to an enormous waste of time. You have to figure out what's best for you and the audience or customer persona you are trying to reach.

I love the story of the fly in the book *you²: A High-Velocity Formula for Multiplying Your Personal Effectiveness in Quantum Leaps* by Price Pritchett. It's a quick read and a must get. Here's Pritchett's introduction to the book:

Here Is a True Story

I'm sitting in a quiet room at the Millcroft Inn, a peaceful little place hidden back among the pine trees about an hour out of Toronto. It's just past noon, late July, and I'm listening to the desperate sounds of a life-or-death struggle going on a few feet away.

There's a small fly burning out the last of its short life's energies in a futile attempt to fly through the glass of the window-pane. The whining wings tell the poignant story of the fly's strategy—try harder.

But it's not working.

The frenzied effort offers no hope for survival. Ironically, the struggle is part of the trap. It is impossible for the fly to try hard enough to succeed at breaking through the glass. Nevertheless, this little insect has staked its life on reaching its goal through raw effort and determination.

This fly is doomed. It will die there on the windowsill.

Across the room, ten steps away, the door is open. Ten seconds of flying time and this small creature could reach the outside world it seeks. With only a fraction of the effort now being wasted, it could be free of this self-imposed trap. The breakthrough possibility is there. It would be so easy.

Why doesn't the fly try another approach, something dramatically different? How did it get so locked in on the idea that this particular route, and determined effort, offer the most promise for success? What logic is there in continuing, until death, to seek a breakthrough with "more of the same"?

No doubt this approach makes sense to the fly. Regrettably, it's an idea that will kill.

"Trying harder" isn't necessarily the solution to achieving more. It may not offer any real promise for getting what you want out of life. Sometimes, in fact, it's a big part of the problem.

If you stake your hopes for a breakthrough on trying harder than ever, you may kill your chances for success.

I probably have reshared this story, not as eloquently of course, hundreds of times. I know my kids have probably heard it a dozen times, but I feel it's something that's just so simple, and yet we don't make a shift to try something new when it's right in front of us.

Stop doing the same things over and over again if you aren't seeing any success from them. If you are going to the same networking events and seeing the same people, you probably won't generate any new potential business. It's simple math. Of course you feel comfortable and want to be around familiar faces, but will that get you to where you are going?

I mentioned before that you should tell your story to all who will listen; well, these familiar people have already heard your story.

Unless you have a new story to tell, you may want to go somewhere else and tell it. That said, BNI groups (and others) are the same people, telling the same stories, week after week after week, but in theory and sometimes in practice, this helps you build an extra team of people spreading the word about your business in the form of referrals. So while I appreciate the impulse to try new venues if you aren't having success in the old ones, it's important to make the distinction between being a regular part of a group that helps bring you referrals and knowing when an event or group is not helping you do that.

I'm not saying to not attend those familiar events, but maybe put an annual limit on how many you plan to attend. In the last two months I have done events in Texas, San Francisco, Maryland, Virginia, Pennsylvania, and Washington, DC, and next month I'm heading to Toronto. If you have a product you can take on the road, do it.

If your business is more locally based, model your ideal client and customers, and spend your time finding where they might be spending their time and whom you might already be connected with to introduce you.

Networking has become an essential skill for professionals in all industries. It involves building connections, fostering relationships, and creating alliances that can lead to new opportunities and professional growth. Let's explore the importance of networking at various types of events (listed below). Additionally, we will delve into the principles of Needworking and connecting on topics while understanding Needs as key aspects of successful networking.

Networking events are meant to bring others together to connect and by chance create mutual opportunities. Needworking can help take the chance out of networking and create synergies and get to the point. Every event you attend may have a different look and feel. Events can be structured as small intimate groups and could feature a lecture or presentation. Other events are larger and more casual to give people time to converse with one another. The purpose of these events is for people in an industry to grow their network. Needworking can help take the guesswork out of the events that you attend to have a greater percentage of matching and the ultimate level of reciprocity.

Here's a list of an eleven different types of events where you can put your networking and Needworking skills to good use:

1. Happy hour meetups
2. Industry-specific seminars
3. Virtual groups
4. Career fairs
5. Conferences/trade shows
6. Breakfast or luncheon meetings
7. Workshops and roundtable discussions
8. Sporting events where decision-makers go
9. Government (state or local) events or ribbon cuttings
10. Golf outings
11. Charity events

Let's take a closer look at each type of event.

1. **Happy Hour Meetups:** Happy hour meetups provide a relaxed and informal setting for professionals to connect after work. These events offer an opportunity to meet people from various industries and build relationships outside of formal settings. Engaging in conversations centered around

shared interests, hobbies, or industry topics can help establish common ground and foster connections. By actively listening and understanding the Needs of others, you can identify potential synergies and opportunities for collaboration.

2. **Industry-Specific Seminars:** Industry-specific seminars gather professionals with a common interest in a particular field. Attending these seminars allows you to connect with individuals who possess specialized knowledge and insights. Engaging in discussions, asking thought-provoking questions, and sharing your expertise all help to demonstrate your passion for the industry. By connecting on topics of mutual interest and understanding the Needs of other professionals, you can establish meaningful connections that may lead to future collaborations or mentorship opportunities.

3. **Virtual Groups:** Virtual groups, such as online communities and forums, provide a platform for professionals to connect, share knowledge, and exchange ideas. Engaging in virtual groups allows you to connect with individuals globally, transcending geographical limitations. By actively participating in discussions, providing valuable insights, and addressing the Needs of others, you can establish yourself as a trusted resource within the community. This builds credibility and opens doors to potential collaborations and partnerships.

4. **Career Fairs:** Career fairs are excellent networking opportunities where professionals from various companies and industries gather. Engaging in conversations with recruiters, decision-makers, and industry experts can help you understand the Needs and requirements of different organizations.

By showcasing your skills, expressing genuine interest in others' work, and understanding their Needs, you can establish connections that may lead to job opportunities, partnerships, or valuable industry insights.

5. **Conferences/Trade Shows:** Conferences and trade shows bring together professionals, industry experts, and thought leaders. Attending these events provides a platform for networking and knowledge sharing. Engaging in conversations and connecting on relevant industry topics allows you to understand the Needs and challenges faced by others. By actively seeking to address those Needs and offering assistance or solutions, you can establish yourself as a valuable resource and build trust among your peers.

6. **Breakfast or Luncheon Meetings:** Breakfast or luncheon meetings offer a more intimate setting for networking and relationship building. These events often feature guest speakers or panel discussions, providing an opportunity to connect on specific topics. By actively participating in discussions, actively listening, and understanding the Needs of others, you can establish meaningful connections. Building rapport and trust in these settings can lay the foundation for potential collaborations, partnerships, or mentorship opportunities.

7. **Workshops and Roundtable Discussions:** Workshops and roundtable discussions foster collaboration, idea sharing, and problem-solving. Engaging in these interactive sessions allows you to connect with professionals who possess expertise in complementary areas. By actively participating, demonstrating your knowledge, and understanding the Needs and challenges faced by others, you can offer valuable insights and

build connections based on mutual understanding. These connections can lead to collaborations that address shared Needs and drive innovation.

8. **Sporting Events Where Decision-Makers Go:** Sporting events provide a relaxed and informal environment for networking. Attending these events, particularly when decision-makers are present, creates opportunities for casual conversations and relationship building. By connecting on shared interests and understanding the Needs of others, you can establish rapport and build trust. These connections may evolve into professional alliances, collaborations, or future business opportunities.

9. **Government (State or Local) Events or Ribbon Cuttings:** Government events (like "state of the city" addresses or ribbon cuttings) provide a platform to connect with influential individuals, including government officials and local leaders. Attending these events demonstrates your support for the community and allows you to engage in conversations centered around shared interests. By understanding the Needs and priorities of the community and offering your expertise or resources, you can build relationships that may lead to partnerships or advocacy efforts.

10. **Golf Outings:** Golf outings have long been recognized as a networking opportunity. Engaging in a round of golf allows for relaxed conversations, shared experiences, and building personal connections. By actively listening, understanding the Needs of others, and offering support or assistance where possible, you can establish rapport and trust. Golf outings

provide an environment conducive to discussing business opportunities, collaborations, or seeking mentorship.

11. **Charity Events:** Charity events offer an opportunity to network while making a positive impact on the community. Attending these events showcases your commitment to social responsibility and attracts like-minded professionals. By connecting on shared values, understanding the Needs of charitable organizations, and offering your skills or resources, you can build meaningful connections that align with your personal and professional goals.

Networking at various events provides opportunities to build connections, foster relationships, and create alliances that can propel your professional growth. By embracing the principles of Needworking and connecting on topics while understanding the Needs of others, you can establish meaningful connections that lead to collaborations, partnerships, and new opportunities. Whether you attend happy hour meetups, industry-specific seminars, virtual groups, or engage in any of the mentioned events, the keys to success include actively listening, offering support, and establishing rapport. Leverage the power of networking to expand your professional network, enhance your industry knowledge, and create lasting alliances that contribute to your success.

You can find these events online through LinkedIn, Eventbrite, and Needworking. As with any other project, you really have to do your research to see what is out there and then attend to see what magic might occur. We have built the Needworking platform to be searchable based on the topics I mentioned previously.

Networking in New Markets

If you are a person who moves from city to city as part of your work, then you already know that you have to spend the time to find quality events to engage with qualified prospects. I have been in Baltimore all my life, and there's a reason why they call it "Smalltimore." Everyone is connected with everyone, and if you aren't now, you will be. I am brand new to the Richmond area, and I can count on one hand how many contacts I have there. This is something that I have to work on and build, and it won't happen overnight. You can't just walk into a new region and expect the same engagement you have in a network system you have spent years developing.

An easy first step in starting your journey in a new market or a market you already know is attending a simple happy hour event.

I attended a happy hour in Richmond that was created by Prospect Blue. This was something I just found on Eventbrite looking for some connections. I met a handful of good potential contacts to help me engage in that market. What was even better is that I didn't have to spend money, since this was an open happy hour sponsored by Prospect Blue. Events will vary as to cost to attend. This was a great way for me to meet quality people in Richmond, but you won't know until you try. Small markets are great for building a strong network.

Conversation Starters

While networking events are ideal for building professional relationships, starting conversations can sometimes be awkward, especially if it's with complete strangers. If you struggle with this, try to find someone you already know at the event or someone who helped organize the event and ask them if they could introduce you to a couple of people.

The people who have organized the event want to make sure their guests are happy and that they will speak favorably about it to others. They hope you will come back for other events in the future, so just ask.

When starting a conversation with someone you've just met, you will want to stay away from conversations that could bring up different opinions on personal agendas, religion, or politics, unless the event is specifically political or religious and the intent is to connect with other like-minded people. At most networking events, your goal is to find a common ground and connect on a deeper level. My one rule is ask, ask some more, ask again, and make sure you listen. Don't just nod in agreement and act like you're listening. Don't make the mistake of launching into a full-blown sales pitch, and try not to talk about yourself too much.

Ask open-ended questions that normally require more than a "yes" or "no" answer. You find out so much about a business and person when you personally invest in the conversation. Now if the person you're talking to answers a question about their role or profession with a broad job title like attorney or accountant, ask some probing questions, like what type of law they practice or who is their typical clientele. You never know where the conversation will go.

The idea is to learn about the people you are conversing with. Here are a few open-ended questions you can use at networking events to get the conversation started:

Don't throw out the normal "So what do you do?" or "Tell me about yourself." Professionals have told their story thousands of times because they've been asked that question thousands of times. Stand out and don't be the same as everyone else.

Get the conversation flowing by asking specific questions:

"What type of business do you run?"
"How long have you been doing this work?"
"Where were you before this position?"
"Who are your ideal clients, and how do you find them?"

Explain what you do and ask them if there was someone or some company you could connect them with, who ideally would that be? (You're trying to find out what they Need.)

If you Need help growing in the industry, ask them if they could be a mentor or if they could refer you to someone who can help you expand your knowledge.

> "Everyone Needs a coach. It doesn't matter
> whether you're a basketball player, a tennis
> player, a gymnast or a bridge player."
>
> **BILL GATES**

Talk about the event. It's only natural to talk about something you're already doing—attending the same event. Ask simple icebreakers that will help you find common ground just by being a detective. Remember, they came to the event for the same reason, and you just Need to find some common ground.

"How did you hear about this event?"

"Have you been to one of these before? How often do they happen?"

"What did you think about the speakers/content/subject?"

"Are you nearby, or did you have to travel far?"

"Do you know the organizer of this event?"

"Do you know a lot of people here?" This is a great question, because this person might be able to connect you with others.

"Would you recommend any other events that might make sense for a business like ours?"

The more you network, the more you'll be able to figure out what resonates with your audience. Just be yourself and have fun meeting others. Remember they are there for the same reason, and you might be able to give them a nugget of information they didn't know.

Sometimes it's difficult to connect with people in a large room, especially if their business roles are all over the place. That's why industry-specific events are great places to find common ground with like-minded people. I would highly recommend that you do your research and find events that have the perfect personas you developed in the last chapter to match what you are trying to accomplish.

Once you find that perfect business persona, do a deeper dive on what events they attend.

For example if you are looking for credit unions as customers, at the top level you can attend an event sponsored by the Credit Union National Association, as well as regional credit union associations.

There is even an association of all the associations: the American Society of Association Executives (ASAE). Take the time to learn about those associations. You can find an association and their regional and national events that might interest you. (See https://www.asaecenter.org/.)

You can't grow and do your business without the help of others, and researching events is a crucial part of networking. As you grow your network and your business and have knowledge of these specific events, let us know and add them to Needworking.com.

Better yet, if you meet an event organizer and you are looking for an icebreaker and they haven't heard about the Needworking process, they will be extremely grateful to you for giving them an opportunity to post their event on the platform and tell a story to an audience they weren't aware of.

The Takeaway

1. **Choose the right events:** With numerous events available, it's crucial to identify which ones align with your goals and target audience. Rather than attending every event, focus on those that offer the best opportunities for reaching your desired persona.

2. **Embrace new approaches:** The story of the fly trapped by a windowpane serves as a reminder to avoid getting stuck in repetitive patterns. Trying harder isn't always

the solution to achieving success. Be open to new approaches, and shift your strategies when necessary.

3. **Expand your horizons:** Continuously attending the same networking events and meeting the same people won't necessarily generate fresh business opportunities. Step outside your comfort zone, explore different events, and connect with unfamiliar faces. Seek out events where your target audience might be present.

4. **Tailor your story:** When networking with people who have already heard your story, make sure you have something new to share. Develop a captivating narrative that highlights your growth, achievements, or industry insights. Engage in conversations that go beyond repetitive introductions.

5. **Event types:** Familiarize yourself with various event types. Each event offers unique networking opportunities.

6. **Needworking principles:** Implement the principles of Needworking, which involve connecting on topics, understanding others' Needs, and fostering reciprocity. Actively listen, ask open-ended questions, and show genuine interest in the person you're conversing with.

7. **Research events:** Utilize platforms like Google, LinkedIn, Eventbrite, and Needworking to discover relevant events. Conduct thorough research to find events that align with your goals and interests. Each platform offers search functionalities to help you find the right events to attend.

8. **Adapt to new markets:** If you're entering a new market or transitioning to a different location, invest time in finding quality events to engage with potential prospects. Building a network takes time, so be patient and persistent in your efforts to establish connections in a new region.

9. **Happy hour as a starting point:** Happy hours can serve as a great first step in entering a new market. Look for open happy hours or events organized by relevant companies or communities. Attend these events to meet quality people and initiate conversations.

10. **Start conversations:** Starting conversations at networking events can be challenging, but there are strategies to make it easier. Avoid controversial topics and focus on finding common ground. Ask open-ended questions, listen attentively, and be genuinely interested in the other person. Avoid dominating the conversation or launching into a full sales pitch.

11. **Icebreaker questions:** Instead of the typical "So, what do you do?" or "Tell me about yourself." questions, ask more specific and engaging questions. Inquire about their business, their experience, their ideal clients, or ask if they Need any specific connections. Be a detective and find common ground.

12. **Talk about the event:** Discussing the event itself can be a natural conversation starter. Ask how they heard about the event, their thoughts on the venue or speakers, or any highlights they've noticed. This

shared experience can help build rapport and initiate further discussions.

By implementing these strategies and attending the right events, you can enhance your networking skills, establish valuable connections, and create opportunities for professional growth. Remember to be open-minded, curious, and focused on building meaningful relationships based on reciprocity and mutual understanding.

"We cannot seek achievement for ourselves and forget about progress and prosperity for our community... Our ambitions must be broad enough to include the aspirations and Needs of others, for their sakes and for our own."

CESAR CHAVEZ

CHAPTER 9

ALIGN WITH ALLIES— DUNBAR'S NUMBERS

Y our network is one of a kind. It's like a fingerprint of who you are and the friends, Allies, Trusted Allies, and cohorts that you keep.

Three Types of Contacts

In the Needworking process, we have three types of contacts you can categorize at the current moment: Allies, Trusted Allies, and cohorts.

Let's delve into the differences and similarities between an ally, a trusted ally, and a cohort within the framework of Needworking principles:

1. **Ally:** An ally in the context of Needworking refers to someone who supports and collaborates with you, often on specific tasks or projects. This person might share common goals or interests with you, and you both work together to achieve those goals. An ally can provide assistance, insights, and resources to help you succeed in your endeavors. This connection might be more task-oriented and focused on immediate objectives.

   Differences from other contacts:

   - An ally might not necessarily have a deep understanding of your broader aspirations or personal values.
   - The level of trust might not be as high as in a trusted ally relationship.
   - The connection might not extend beyond the specific tasks or projects you collaborate on.

   Similarities with other contacts:

   - Both an ally and a trusted ally involve collaboration and support towards common goals.
   - Both types of connections contribute to expanding your network and resources.

2. **Trusted Ally:** A trusted ally goes beyond the role of a regular ally. This type of connection is built on a foundation of trust and a deeper understanding of each other's Needs, values, and long-term objectives. A trusted ally is someone you can confide in, share your challenges and aspirations with, and rely on for guidance and support in various aspects of your

life. This connection is more holistic and is based on a mutual commitment to each other's growth and success.

Differences from other contacts:

◻   A trusted ally relationship involves a higher level of trust and understanding compared to one with a regular ally.

◻   The scope of collaboration extends beyond specific tasks or projects to encompass a broader range of life and career aspects.

◻   The relationship with a trusted ally is characterized by deeper emotional investment and support.

Similarities with other contacts:

◻   Like an ally, a trusted ally also involves collaboration and mutual support.

3. **Cohort:** A cohort, in the context of Needworking, refers to a group of individuals who share common interests, goals, or experiences. This group can serve as a support system, providing a sense of belonging and camaraderie. Cohorts often engage in collective activities, discussions, and initiatives that align with their shared interests. Being part of a cohort can offer diverse perspectives, resources, and opportunities for personal and professional growth.

Differences from other contacts:

◻   A cohort involves a collective dynamic where multiple individuals contribute to each other's growth.

- ▫ Cohorts tend to have a broader focus on shared interests rather than individual Needs.
- ▫ The connection within a cohort is influenced by group dynamics and interactions.

Similarities with other contacts:

- ▫ Similar to Allies and Trusted Allies, cohorts also provide a support network and opportunities for collaboration.
- ▫ All three types of connections contribute to expanding your network and enhancing your personal and professional life.

Basically, an ally is a collaborator who assists with specific tasks; a trusted ally is a deeper, more comprehensive connection based on mutual trust and understanding; and a cohort is a group of individuals who share common interests and goals. Each type of connection, while distinct, plays a role in building a well-rounded network that can help you meet a variety of personal and professional Needs based on the principles of Needworking.

That being said, a cohort is a type of group, but not all groups are cohorts. Cohorts are often formed around a common bond or purpose and can include individuals from various backgrounds who come together for a specific reason. For example, a cohort of students entering a program together, a cohort of professionals in the same industry, or a cohort of people with similar life experiences can all exist.

In essence, all cohorts are groups, but not all groups are cohorts. Cohorts are a specific subset of groups that emphasize a closer connection based on shared characteristics or experiences. So, while the terms are related, "cohort" often implies a more specialized and focused form of group.

Think back to when you first opened your Facebook, Instagram, or LinkedIn account. You connected with people who were in your circles and then connected with people in their circles, and eventually you reached another ring. As time continues, and if you don't delete connections, pretty soon you have compounding people. Compounding can be a great thing, especially when it comes to investing. As part of the Goldman Sachs 10KSB, our group has had several interactions with Mr. Warren Buffett. Now in his nineties, he is still brilliant and is filled with a tremendous amount of wisdom.

Warren Buffett was so excited when he realized the power of compounding interest, allowing money and investments that just grew and grew over time. Albert Einstein famously called it "the eighth wonder of the world" and noted, "He who understands it, earns it ... he who doesn't ... pays it." If you have a chance to watch the documentary *Becoming Warren Buffett*, it's fascinating to see how the Oracle of Omaha pays for his morning breakfast at McDonald's, a company he's well vested in.

Compounding interest and compounding knowledge are two of the best things you can do. This is not only investing for personal wealth, but for personal growth as well.

However, compounding isn't the greatest strategy for growing a personal network of trusted people, unless of course you are growing a fan base on social platforms. It's fascinating to watch how TikTok, Instagram, LinkedIn, and Facebook are expanding, especially as people are creating content to increase their followings. As I mentioned before, the landscape has become a whole new way of using mass media.

Besides a number, what are you actually getting from these followers? Are you learning from them, collaborating with them, or just performing for them? How much time have you invested in creating videos and other content? These too are products that will compound interest as long as the platforms you post stay relevant. The problem will be content overload, and your content game will have to keep up the pace and generate more attention than the other pieces. As you build and grow this form of network, it's difficult to build Allies you can turn to, and it will be a never-ending game growing your audience and possibly disappointment if followers unfollow.

So building an audience is one way, but how do you build Allies that you can turn to, and on the flip side, who can turn to you?

You've probably seen the many quotes about whom to surround yourself with. Just search "Surround Yourself Quotes", and you will find hundreds of people who have modeled this behavior to live their lives.

> "Surround yourself with only people who are going to lift you higher."
> **OPRAH WINFREY**

> "You can't build any kind of organization if you're not going to surround yourself with people who have experience and skill base beyond your own."
> **HOWARD SCHULTZ**

> "Don't let people disrespect you. My mom says don't open the door to the devil. Surround yourself with positive people."
> **CUBA GOODING JR.**

"I always tell young girls, surround
yourself with goodness. I learned early on
how to get the haters out of my life."
MICHELLE OBAMA

"Success is not a solo journey; it's a collective
effort. Surround yourself with supportive
people who inspire and uplift you."
DAVE CARBERRY

This message about surrounding yourself with great people is a principle people live by. Have you ever been in a situation where you looked around at the crowd you were hanging out with and realized, "This is a place and time I don't belong"? You go with the group and it ends up in regret for you. If that's currently happening to you, PIVOT! Yes, I'm saying that in Ross' voice from the TV show *Friends*.

Don't stay in that position, and get rid of the negativity/situation you are in that Needs to be altered. In other words, "Don't let the clowns bring you down." You want a group of inspiring individuals that takes you to new heights. I will discuss groups later, but I can't stress enough the importance of finding a good group that could use your knowledge and a group that will provide you with constructive feedback and advice.

When I was a teenager and early in my career, I loved absorbing business leadership books, although I wish I had known sooner about Warren Buffett and Berkshire Hathaway. Reading about and exploring ways to connect in business, along with taking a Dale Carnegie course, really built my structure on how to have conversations with people who were my elders in business. It was a great entry into learning a style of communication that helped propel me in my career. Here are just ten of the thirty principles Carnegie wrote about in his book *How To Win Friends and Influence People*:

1. Don't Criticize, Condemn, Or Complain

2. Give Honest, Sincere Appreciation

3. Arouse In The Other Person An Eager Want

4. Become Genuinely Interested In Other People

5. Smile

6. Remember That A Person's Name Is To That Person The Sweetest And Most Important Sound In Any Language

7. Be A Good Listener. Encourage Others To Talk About Themselves

8. Talk In Terms Of The Other Person's Interests

9. Make The Other Person Feel Important— And Do It Sincerely

10. The Only Way To Get The Best Of An Argument Is To Avoid It

Now if you take all of his principles and let's say match them up with your LinkedIn, Instagram, and TikTok followers, how many items in the list could relate to the audience you are producing content for? Maybe you can provide some advice to someone, but you may not have a personal engagement with someone.

I recently saw a post on LinkedIn from a friend of mine, Kait LeDonne, who wrote:

> "No one really cares about you" is probably the best, most direct advice I can give to people looking to build their brand.
>
> Why don't they care about you?
>
> Because they're too busy caring about THEMSELVES.

At first I thought, she's wrong. People do care, I believe in people, and the people that I've surrounded myself with are caring humans. I was ready to pounce on this post and argue with her about that. I stopped because first off I don't want to be that negative curmudgeon that pooh-poohs someone's ideas for their own journey.

I rethought it, and in hindsight, she has a point. People who don't care probably are the people you don't want to align yourself with. People don't care about the vacation you are posting on LinkedIn if they really don't know you. People don't care about the event you attended unless it had relevance to them attending.

People you don't have a meaningful connection with won't care as much as a person with a deeper connection to you. Aligning yourself to others is crucial, and having thousands of connections isn't really the way to surround yourself with people.

Needworking was built with that in mind. You can have as many connections as you want, but you have the option to categorize your contacts as Allies or Trusted Allies. I just love the term Allies and what it represents. The definition is a person, group, or nation that is associated with another or others for some common cause or purpose.

Your Trusted Allies will help you with your purpose and your cause as long as they believe and trust in what you are doing. You don't Need thousands of followers, but having and surrounding yourself with people who can support you and you in turn can support them is essential to us moving forward as a society.

Professor Robin Dunbar gave a 2012 TED Talk entitled, "Why the Internet Won't Get You Any More Friends." Dunbar, an anthropologist and evolutionary psychologist, does a breakdown on how many friends and acquaintances we can actually be connected to at any given moment.

Think about the close friends you've kept over the years, and think about the friends who have just fallen by the wayside. We all have times in our lives where we shed friends based on the situation. It could have been a move, a lost love or a new love, so-called friends who talked behind your back or held vastly opposing political views. It's okay; there are lots of people in this world, and you Need to find the tribe that you feel safe and secure with.

Dunbar has also gone on to write books on the subject of friendship, including *Friends: Understanding the Power of Our Most Important Relationships* and *How Many Friends Does One Person Need? Dunbar's Number and Other Evolutionary Quirks.* Dunbar's number is the number of meaningful and stable relationships you can have at any one time. That includes extended family as well as friends. Dunbar explains that people who come from large extended families have fewer friends because they give priority to family members. The number 150 is an average, but there's a lot of variation. The range of variation is somewhere between 100 and 250.

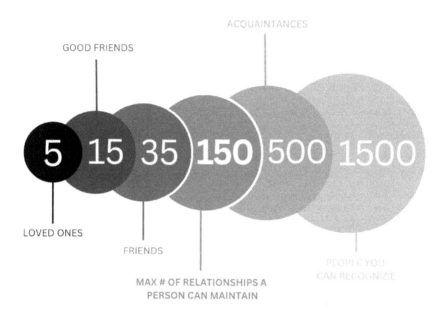

Dunbar's studies have focused primarily on individuals and their friends and not as much on business relationships. The principal idea is that your intimate interaction is your life partner or someone who is the closest to you. Close friends are those who would drop everything to support and be there for you, in good or bad times. The circle of fifteen encompasses those you spend the most time with and enjoy moments together. Each range represents a different level of connection and yes, we can see thousands of people connected to us, but how many are truly having reciprocal forms of communication? This is not a simple "like" or a comment on your social media pages. This could be in the form of a personal text, a Zoom call, a face-to-face get-together, or a call. What is the percentage of your current connections that you have met with in the last thirty days or even the past year?

Your business/professional connections could be very different from your personal connections, and therefore you almost should have two versions of Dunbar's number that represent your connections. I would say your intimates might be the same, especially if your spouse is your business partner. After that, any of those circles can be modified and altered based on your relationships. You might have close friends who aren't in your line of work and can't relate to your profession. You may have work acquaintances, Allies, and groups you are in that you spend more time with than you do family.

Just think about that list from Dale Carnegie, and now try to imagine how to build out your circles. You might have clients you are close to, but you keep them at arm's length, to ensure that you are providing extremely professional services and not spending personal time with them. In some cases, your client might be someone who is extremely close to you, and the relationship has been successful, and you both have grown greatly from that interaction, personally and professionally.

There are many out there who try to debunk theories and research with their own research and learning. Scott Barry Kaufman redefines Maslow's Hierarchy in his book *Transcend: The New Science of Self-Actualization*. He pulls apart the hierarchy theory and reduces the pyramid shape to resemble the Needs being more like a sailboat. His theory is that the winds of change happen, and you don't necessarily stack the Needs in a hierarchical order but focus on the Needs at the moment of occurrence.

There are also many who try to debunk Dunbar's number, but it isn't exact, and Dunbar is very matter-of-fact that it's a general number that varies based on connections and experiences. We believe that there are ranges and numbers of connections that are ideal to build your network. As we gather more data on connections, we can better determine in the future the ideal ranges. It won't be an exact science since there are other tools like LinkedIn and Slack that have varying ways to connect. We have launched the Needworking platform to have a few simple ways to connect with people while trying to alleviate the spammy feeling you get from being on other platforms.

We believe that as you grow your network and your relationships, you can't have an intimate connection with thousands of people. At the moment of this writing, I have 5,938 followers and 5,678 first-level connections on LinkedIn. I just took a glance at the first fifty of those connections and I had to re-familiarize myself with how I knew them. I had to review their title, company, and location. I then clicked on well over 35% to gain more insight with those I wasn't familiar with. You should try this exercise as well. How many first-level connections do you have that aren't really first-level priority?

LinkedIn and other platforms have added features that entice you to keep coming back and growing your network. Needworking of course will add features that will encourage people to act within the platform. We have been trained to react emotionally when activities happen. LinkedIn congratulates you when you have a new connection, as they should. It's awesome to connect to people and grow your network. The key is where will those connections be when you really Need them?

I'll admit it—I'm a little headstrong! Who in their right mind would create and build a social network, when there are already lots of ways to connect online? It seems like an insurmountable task. In reality it's hard, but not impossible. I have been friends with people for many years, and I've been shouting on every social platform that I have built this brand-new platform: "Please come and check it out. Come in and post the nonprofit events you are hosting. Come start a group, come post you are looking for work, just share what you Need or how you can help others."

What has amazed me is that if you look at Dunbar's circle of best friends, I know there are close friends, friends, and even family that haven't even tried to explore the project that I have started. It really tells you a lot about the acquaintances you keep. I understand that people have busy schedules, and they might not like to be on social media, but given the number of people that I am connected with on Facebook and LinkedIn, you would think the people that are closest to you would take the time. I'm not asking them to travel to a destination wedding; I'm asking them to look at my work at a destination that they visit from the comfort of their own home. I will also step up and say perhaps my messaging to them could be clearer about the benefits of the platform and its relevance to them.

What has been incredible is the number of people who have started to use the platform as it's meant to be and are consistent users. I have met so many new people in this journey who I wasn't expecting to be in my circle of core users and who are now friends. These amazing users were in my circle of acquaintances before, but I've become closer to them and understand their business and Needs even more.

You are less likely to see a feed about business accomplishments or graduations on Needworking. Because of that, the number of topic-based posts that you might see in a day is far less than what might be on another platform. When you have a feed that includes over 5,000 connections, it can be overwhelming to keep up with the posts. In the Needworking and social media scenario, less is often more.

Needworking doesn't want to be the next LinkedIn or Facebook. We want to ensure people are slimming down and reconnecting with their Connections, Allies and Trusted Allies. We allow for you to connect and label your connections either to send messages or just simply remind you that you should be connecting with your Allies on a more regular basis.

We also alert your connection that you've been added as a Trusted Ally. This provides acknowledgement to your Ally that they are more than just a regular connection and that you value the relationship.

In the book *Superconnector*, Scott Gerber and Ryan Paugh talk about the addiction factor that is part of these social platforms and the fear of missing out (FOMO) they create. I love this quote from *Superconnector*: "If you focus on building fans and followers on social media, regularly share content using 'inbound marketing' techniques, and attend networking events, you will be able to amass a giant network from which to extract the value—and win at big business. Never mind the time and care it takes to get to know the actual people you meet; you can just 'growth hack' your way to Rolodex success." They continue, "It's exhausting just reading it. Here's the truth: The number of contacts and followers you have online does not trump real relationships. Being virtually or offline 'connected' is not in itself valuable. Social capital cannot be measured in likes and shares. Instead, you have to acquire social capital and build trust and meaningful relationships through the right conversations, actions and value exchange with the right people."

The bottom line is the more people who are trying to get your attention, the less space and time you have in your head for real-life situations. If everyone else is using social media sites, and if someone doesn't join in, there's concern that they'll miss events or invitations, possible connection opportunities, or invitations. Missing experiences can create anxiety and longing to belong. When people look online and see they're excluded or even just missed an opportunity, it can affect thoughts and feelings, and even affect them physically.

If you haven't watched the Netflix Original *The Social Dilemma*, you should. It digs deep into the logic and algorithms that Facebook has developed to keep people hooked on social media content. If you really think about it, this is also a dilemma that any business owner, publisher, or salesperson must contend with. How do you keep people coming back? Facebook knowingly has created a systematic way to create demand on the platform; this includes Instagram. In her 2021 testimony in front of a Senate Committee on Commerce, Science, & Transportation, "Protecting Kids Online: Testimony from a Facebook Whistleblower," former data scientist at Facebook Frances Haugen revealed that her former employer is knowingly harmful to children, promotes divisiveness among users, and amplifies misinformation in pursuit of growth and what she calls "astronomical profits."

According to the Pew Research Center, 89% of teens have a smartphone, and studies have shown that young people are spending up to nine hours on social media and digital technology, posting pictures, streaming videos, and listening to music daily. We are a connected world online but disconnected with humans in deeper, meaningful ways. Years ago I called it "socialization isolation." We can be sitting in a room full of people or with family, and everyone is on their phones, but not communicating with one another in person.

We are compounding people, compounding brain stimulation, compounding societal complexities. Our brains are soaking up more media and being fed more content than ever before. LOOK, SQUIRREL!

I can't say I have a solution for this, but I can say I'd like to try to offer something that is a pace slower than the other feed-filled platforms you find. The Needworking algorithm is based primarily on the topics you choose. You have five topics that you can follow and that flow into your feed. You can pick fewer to slow down the feed, and you can pick more for a charge.

We will intertwine your Allies' and Trusted Allies' Needs into your feed, but we want to slow down the amount of noise and create an algorithm that is chosen by you. As we grow, you make the choices as to what your feed and feedback will be.

When you post a Need, you can also send it to anyone—your connections or just your Allies and Trusted Allies. I realize this isn't a revolutionary feature. When it launched, Facebook utilized, and still does to this day, a way for you to send messages to your friends, or pick and choose what friends to exclude. Facebook also set their advertising console to allow for this targeting. Running an ad, you can choose to target people who have liked your business as well as their friends. The assumption is that birds of a feather flock together.

There is nothing wrong with flocking together; you just have to find the right flock and make sure it's flying in the same direction as you are planning to travel. The key is spending the time to bring together the people that make up your circle, and it's unique to only you. There is no other network of people that identically matches yours. You Need to protect that network and the people that are in it. Listen to them and help them every opportunity you can.

Dunbar has written several books on his studies regarding the brain and connecting and circles of friendship. In *Understanding The Power of Our Most Important Relationships*, he builds out what he calls the Seven Pillars of Friendship:

- ➜ Having the same language (dialect)
- ➜ Growing up in the same location
- ➜ Having had the same educational and career experiences (medical people gravitate together, and lawyers do the same)
- ➜ Having the same hobbies or interests
- ➜ Having the same world view (an amalgam of moral views, religious views, and political views)
- ➜ Having the same sense of humor
- ➜ Having the same musical tastes

I can see where this is completely on point when it comes to personal relationships, but when it comes to business, how do these relationships still fall into place?

Dunbar goes on to describe that the groupings of these pillars go on to create small communities, and typically those communities are around 150 people and can be considered an extended family of sorts. I have friends/connections that group together and follow the band Phish from city to city. Personally I can't get into their music (sorry Phish fans), but I do love seeing the posts and how tight-knit they are. I'm sure they have grown a unique camaraderie and bond from spending time together at the event and possibly after.

I'm not here to tell you that you Need to limit yourself and connections to under 250 or under 2,500 for that matter. I just want to stress the importance of connecting on a deeper level and spending the necessary time to build a connection. We all can't be Tony Robbins or Gary Vaynerchuk and drop videos and drop f-bombs to build a huge audience base. Some of us aren't built for putting our personalities out there like that. They are in a community all their own. Being comfortable in the communities you are in and having a reciprocal relationship is the key to your networking or Needworking success.

Jay Shetty also speaks to four stages of trust, a key element of building a network:

1. **Neutral Trust:** Positive qualities of that person exist, but that does not merit trust, especially with someone new.
2. **Contractual Trust:** You scratch my back, I'll scratch yours.
3. **Mutual:** Help goes both ways; you know you'll be there for one another in the future.
4. **Pure:** No matter what happens, you'll have one another's back.

In my theories about Allies, we are all interconnected based on our Needs and Maslow's hierarchy on how we can help one another. Shetty feels that there is a pyramid of trust relationships that you have with others. This can also be adjacent to Dunbar's number and how people can stay on that pyramid or fall off. Safety is a Need, and Shetty states it's okay and necessary, in fact, to protect yourself from those who aren't good for you.

If you circle back to the Needworking hierarchical pyramid in chapter 5, you could also intersect Dunbar's numbers with Maslow's Needs to be the culmination of what Needworking really is.

At the pinnacle of the combined hierarchy, where the Networking hierarchy and Maslow's hierarchy of Needs intersect, truly resonates with the human connection—Reciprocity. This stage is reminiscent of Dunbar's number theory, which suggests that humans can maintain stable relationships with around 150 individuals due to cognitive and social limitations.

In the context of the Networking hierarchy, Reciprocity is the realization of symbiotic networking relationships, where the exchange of value and support becomes a cornerstone. Just as Dunbar's number emphasizes the limits of meaningful relationships, Reciprocity signifies a deliberate and purposeful engagement with a select few—individuals who have evolved from Trusted Allies to become a core circle.

Within this intimate circle, akin to Dunbar's theorized "inner circle," the essence of reciprocity is magnified. The exchange of knowledge, resources, and opportunities becomes more profound due to the established trust and shared objectives. This interdependence is characterized by a genuine commitment to one another's growth and prosperity.

Dunbar's number theory reinforces the idea that even in the expansive realm of networking, the depth of relationships often takes precedence over sheer quantity. Just as Maslow's self-transcendence stage signifies a broader sense of connection with humanity,

Dunbar's concept speaks to the depth and authenticity of connections within one's inner circle.

Incorporating Dunbar's number theory into the Apex of the combined hierarchy adds a layer of psychological insight to the reciprocity stage. It underscores the understanding that even as networking expands and flourishes, the most profound impact often arises from the concentrated energy directed towards a select group—a group nurtured through trust, shared objectives, and the principles of reciprocity. This fusion of concepts encapsulates the pinnacle of both personal development and networking accomplishments.

The Takeaway

Building a strong network of Allies is crucial for your personal growth and success. While social media platforms offer a wide reach, the true value lies in meaningful connections rather than amassing a large number of followers. Quality trumps quantity when it comes to building a network of trusted individuals who can support and collaborate with you.

Surrounding yourself with great people is a principle many successful individuals live by. It's important to evaluate the company you keep and ensure that they inspire and uplift you. If you find yourself in a negative or unproductive environment, it's essential to pivot and seek out a tribe that aligns with your values and goals.

Learning effective communication skills, such as those outlined in Dale Carnegie's principles, can greatly enhance your ability to connect with others. However, when considering your online audience, it's important to recognize that not everyone will care deeply about your content unless there is a personal connection or relevance to their own interests.

Robin Dunbar's research on friendship highlights the limitations of the number of meaningful relationships we can maintain at a given time. While Dunbar primarily focused on personal friendships, it's worth considering how these circles of connection apply to professional relationships as well. Your business network may differ from your personal circle, and it's important to identify which connections hold priority in your life.

In the age of social media, where platforms encourage constant growth and engagement, it's crucial to consider where your connections will be when you truly Need them. Needworking provides a valuable solution by prioritizing authentic connections and facilitating meaningful interactions. By leveraging the platform, you can focus on cultivating relationships with individuals who believe in your purpose and are willing to support you. This ensures that your network consists of true Allies and Trusted Allies who can make a meaningful impact on your personal and professional journey.

CHAPTER 10

BE INCLUSIVE WITH GROUPS AND ALLIES

When we started creating the Needworking process, we were working off the Babson College curriculum topics in 10,000 Small Businesses. The list was relatively small, with maybe around forty topics at the most. These topics or categories included the coursework we utilized to work on our growth opportunity. The coursework was centered on topics like accounting, marketing, employment, training, technology, and mostly top-level areas of expertise. We also discussed diversity and inclusion as part of our learning and ways to bid on government contracts and much more.

Our group was actually called Baltimore Cohort #4, and the people who made up our cohort were extremely diverse. Not only were they diverse in terms of race/gender, but the areas of expertise were just great to be around to see how I could help other business owners and how they could help our organization.

I really have to hand it to Goldman Sachs and Bloomberg Philanthropies for creating this program. I have made incredible Allies with this program and learned about businesses that I really wouldn't have connected with otherwise. Caroline Presburg has a company called Bay Runner, which is a shuttle service that takes people from the BWI Airport in the Baltimore/Washington area and transports them to the beaches and shore three hours away, or vice versa. Deepa Srinivasan has an emergency management company for cities and municipalities across the United States. Robin Belle has a home healthcare company called Road Runner. I could go on and on, but the great thing is we all are dealing with day-to-day business issues. In the last chapter I wrote about Dunbar's seven pillars of friendship. This is why friendship and business can mesh, but the pillars don't always align.

Our cohort came from different backgrounds and went to different schools. We didn't have anyone that we were really connected with previously, and we had no idea what our hobbies or interests were. We just all knew we were in it together and running our own companies. I went in thinking I had some great experience and knowledge about business and realized I knew marketing and advertising really well but had a lot to learn about the other aspects of running my company, from employee handbooks to 401(k) plans and software that we should have been using.

Our collective group came together and helped one another simply by digging deeper into each one of our businesses and coming up with ideas, suggestions, and solutions. What we all came together on were the topics. Each one of us had to deal with those top-level topics on a daily basis, and we all had opinions and experiences to share on these topics.

The reason I bring this up is because it's inclusion at the best level. We were all walks of life coming together to help one another and create a strong core of knowledge for one another. The key is coming back together after an event like that and reconnecting. We try to reconnect two to three times a year now, if not in person, then on Zoom.

I agree with Dunbar and how you make up your friends and Allies from the seven pillars, and to that I would expand or even dive deeper into his career and interests pillars. I would explore a connection on topics which could be the same as an interest, but now these interests/topics can be categorized. We come together as a community on topics, whether it be sports, business, health, hobbies, or entertainment. Our families, groups, and Allies get closer when they can relate to things they are passionate about.

I recently ran an advertising campaign promoting Needworking supporting an event in Baltimore that was sending aid to Ukraine. It was an event I felt many would come together to support. There was a tremendous amount of support and tons of negativity surrounding it. The responses/comments were horrific and full of hate. Don't these people realize you can click on their profile and see who is spewing out vulgarity and hate language?

A term that I've been seeing more recently is psychological safety. Our social media platforms are not the safest place to feel included in conversations, especially if you have a different political view or look and act differently. The images and hype that you see on social media can also be far from reality. Platforms allow freedom of expression and speech but also provide an opportunity for open feedback, and that could be dangerous and hurtful. Safety is one Need that Maslow deemed important, and social media can sometimes expose us.

Dr. Timothy Clark, founder and CEO of LeaderFactor, wrote and developed *The Four Stages of Psychological Safety: Defining the Path to Inclusion and Innovation.*

Clark is a global expert in the fields of senior executive development, strategy acceleration, and organizational change.

Clark's Four Stages of Psychological Safety

Stage 1: Inclusion safety. This level of safety refers to satisfying the basic human Need of connecting and belonging. In this first stage, you feel safe and accepted to be who you are — quirky characteristics and all.

Stage 2: Learner safety. In this stage, you feel safe to learn, ask questions, and experiment. You feel open to giving and receiving feedback (and you even feel safe to make mistakes).

Stage 3: Contributor safety. At this point, you finally feel safe to make a valuable contribution using your skills and gifts.

Stage 4: Challenger safety. This final stage involves feeling safe enough to challenge the status quo when you see an opportunity for change or improvement. According to Clark, team members must progress through these stages in order to feel comfortable enough to speak up and make valuable contributions.

Clark's book focuses on the workplace primarily, but you can apply this same safety factor to social media. People want to feel secure and included, especially when they are completely vulnerable.

The way social media circles work now is based on people that you know and then people that they know. It's like the "Six Degrees of Kevin Bacon" game. You start with yourself and the network of people you have grown to be around you and expand that network. Typically the diversity in that network is weak. Again, if we are evaluating Dunbar's seven pillars of friendship, it's based on our experiences. Unbeknownst to many of us, people get judged and attacked on a regular basis.

I know I am a rainbows-and-unicorns kind of thinker and believe that people are coming together and things aren't like they were in the 1950s and '60s, but there is a great divide. You see it on our nightly news when people are getting shot and killed in metropolitan cities, and without hesitation you stereotype who did the shooting and who got shot. The reality is you don't know, but you assume. We were not born with stereotyping; it was learned.

Psychologists call our mental shortcuts heuristics. Heuristics are mental shortcuts that allow people to solve problems and make judgments quickly and efficiently.

But heuristics can lead us down a rabbit hole to make potentially damaging assumptions about others. Typically, the most common discussion is that of racial stereotyping. Racial stereotyping comes from the belief that membership in a racial group defines someone on a range of characteristics. Behavior and a group's beliefs will also be judged.

I personally do not feel that this is limited to race. You could be judged by religion, political party, your country of origin, your clothes, your tattoos, and even the groups you belong to. We judge other people, and it's as simple as that. The key is how to flip the switch on what you normally do and how your heuristic thinking could be switched to a complex thought and go beyond what your mind is telling you.

When I attended the GrowCo event in 2014, I sat in a room of thousands and heard Mark Cuban call himself a bigot. At first it was a shocker that someone of his influence would make a statement like this. Cuban said, "If I see a black kid in a hoodie on my side of the street, I'll move to the other side of the street. If I see a white guy with a shaved head and tattoos [on the side he now is on], I'll move back to the other side of the street. None of us have pure thoughts; we all live in glass houses." The judgment of Mr. Cuban was on high alert in the room. That judgment grew by the public as media outlets were casting stones at him over the next few weeks. This was an opportunity for the media (broadcast and social) to take a deep look at what they do as well. The reporters who covered the story pointed fingers at him, but did they look at their own selves when they wrote those stories? He wasn't wrong, and his intention was for us to all look at ourselves and look at our actions on a daily basis.

We create our own stereotypes because of our own experiences, and those experiences might be limited to the company we keep. We Need to expand our thinking and talk to others from around the world and outside of our comfort zone. We Need to be aware that some degree of bias is inevitable, whether in our own thinking or in the media and social media we are exposed to, and that we Need to be aware of how these shape our thinking.

The key to being inclusive is to bring people together and have no judgment towards others and connect on that topic or interest.

Take a look at your close connections on Facebook or LinkedIn. Are they diverse? Are you learning more about other people to expand your knowledge base of their communities?

Inclusion is also about being heard and taken seriously, and feeling accepted enough in the group or organization to raise different ideas and offer different perspectives.

Fulfilling a Need is often communicated in a way that sounds like you're doing a favor for someone else. However, we feel it can be more easily translated as developing an intentional relationship with others which centers around respect, kindness, caring, and empathy. Being in community with one another requires action, intentionality, and grace for others. We are all learning every day. It's important for each and every one of us to try to understand the experiences of others that are different from our own.

At SXSW I saw Melinda Briana Epler, a TEDx speaker, discuss the concept of being an ally to others, which she extensively covers in her book *How to Be an Ally: Actions You Can Take for a Stronger, Happier Workplace*. Epler used the terms microaggression and microaffirmations during her talk. Microaggressions refer to subtle and often unintentional comments or actions that express prejudice towards marginalized groups. On the other hand, microaffirmations are small gestures that affirm someone's identity, validate their experiences, and support them in their careers.

I believe you not only can look at this from the workplace point of view but also when you are communicating on social media platforms.

Epler provided several suggestions for practicing microaffirmations. Firstly, it's important to build relationships, showing genuine curiosity and compassion towards others' lives and work. Actively listening and being present when others are speaking, and demonstrating empathy and compassion when they share their ideas or experiences are key aspects of being an ally.

Encouraging participation from everyone is a crucial microaffirmation. Actively soliciting ideas and feedback, and creating an inclusive environment where everyone feels comfortable sharing their thoughts, can help mitigate feelings of marginalization or exclusion.

In cases where individuals may be hesitant to participate, it's important to take notice and offer support. People who feel marginalized or like impostors may refrain from contributing, and it's essential to reach out and inquire about ways to assist them.

Inviting someone to speak and share their expertise is another microaffirmation. Whether in speeches, presentations, or corporate events, offering opportunities to individuals who are not often asked to speak can contribute to a more inclusive environment. It's important to ensure equitable compensation for their expertise, especially when the event generates profit.

Overall, as Epler explains, microaffirmations are intentional actions that recognize and validate individuals' identities and experiences, foster inclusion and belonging, and counteract biases and inequities in the workplace. By practicing these small but meaningful gestures, one can contribute to a stronger, happier workplace for everyone.

Even on a video call or in a meeting when you're not speaking, your facial expressions and body language can be an important source of feedback for others. Make sure you are fully present when someone is sharing, and think about the message you're conveying nonverbally. You can nod, show you're thinking and taking in their ideas, indicate you want to know more, let them know you're confused by one of their points, and so on.

The recommendations Epler has provided are not just for the workplace. You can use them on social media platforms, at networking events, or group meetings outside of work. You could even just compliment someone uniquely different in the grocery store or at church.

Needworking tries to eliminate the divide by connecting people on the Topics first and then by Allies and Groups. A diverse group of people could connect on a topic like payroll, whereas if you post a payroll question on Facebook, you might get limited responses. The key is building that trust and reconnecting with someone after the first initial interaction.

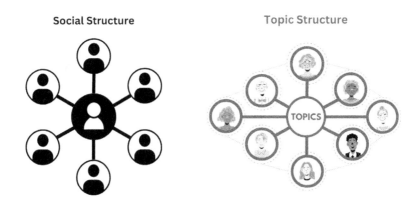

As it's been stated before, it's a benefit to your own health to help someone else, and sometimes it's just as simple as a smile to brighten someone's day, no matter what your heuristics are thinking.

The Takeaway

1. Inclusion and diversity are essential for fostering growth and learning. The diverse backgrounds and areas of expertise within a group can provide valuable insights and support for individuals.

2. Building connections and alliances with others can lead to new opportunities and expand your knowledge base. Collaborating with people from different industries and backgrounds can help you gain unique perspectives and insights into various topics.

3. Psychological safety plays a crucial role in creating inclusive environments, whether in the workplace or on social media platforms. The four stages of psychological safety (inclusion, learner, contributor, and challenger safety) can help individuals feel secure, valued, and able to contribute their ideas and perspectives.

4. Stereotyping is a common tendency that can lead to assumptions and biases. It is important to challenge these stereotypes and engage in complex thinking to go beyond initial judgments. Expanding interactions with diverse communities and embracing different perspectives can help break down stereotypes.

5. Media and social media platforms have a significant influence on shaping people's thinking and perceptions. It is important to critically evaluate the information presented and be aware of potential biases and hidden agendas.

6. Building empathy and understanding among individuals can lead to positive social change.

7. Being inclusive involves connecting with others based on shared interests and topics, without judgment or bias. Actively seeking diverse connections and engaging in regular interactions with individuals from different communities can broaden your understanding and contribute to a more inclusive society.

8. Fulfilling a Need should be seen as developing intentional relationships based on respect, kindness, caring, and empathy. It goes beyond simply doing favors and involves being in community with others and supporting them in meaningful ways.

CHAPTER 11

THE NEEDWORKING PROCESS— RECIPROCITY

As we noted in chapter 3, Abraham Maslow eventually reconceptualized his hierarchy of Needs to have "transcendence" at the top of the pyramid rather than "self-actualization." Part of transcendence is learning to give back after we have accomplished whatever we have set out to achieve.

Doing the research for this book, I never realized how many books existed on the topic of giving back. I thought I was the only one seeing the correlation of Maslow and social media platforms, but to my delight, there are so many prolific writers and storytellers who have studied and proven the power of giving back.

There have been many studies on the health benefits of giving. A 2016 study by S.K. Nelson et al., "Do unto others or treat yourself?

The effects of prosocial and self-focused behavior on psychological flourishing," investigated the impact of different types of behavior on happiness. While popular culture promotes self-focused actions for happiness, the study found that engaging in acts of kindness for others (prosocial behavior) consistently led to greater improvements in psychological well-being than self-oriented actions. Prosocial behavior increased positive emotions and reduced negative emotions, contributing to higher psychological flourishing. In contrast, self-focused behavior did not improve well-being, challenging the idea that self-centered actions are the best route to happiness. The study suggests that focusing on helping others rather than oneself might be a more effective strategy for enhancing happiness.

Other studies have shown regular volunteering can lead to increased life expectancy, enhancing the immune system, lowered cholesterol, and generally reduces stress.

In their book *The Power of Giving*, Azim Jamal and Harvey McKinnon write about the benefits of giving as well as identifying what you can give that might make others happy and yourself satisfied. We all have gifts, and we should be sharing them with others, no matter how big or small. Jamal and McKinnon mention simple things like sharing vegetables from the garden or calling a relative to say hello. Simple things can go a long way. They dig into thirteen things that you can give that could make a difference in someone's life, including your own:

➜   love
➜   laughter
➜   knowledge
➜   leadership

- ➜ hope
- ➜ life
- ➜ time
- ➜ money
- ➜ skills
- ➜ health
- ➜ touch
- ➜ attention
- ➜ advice

Many of these go hand in hand. You can't give hope without it coming from a place of love. You use your time to learn and then give that time and knowledge back to others.

We have tried to harness the power of technology to be able to make it easier for others to be able to share these gifts with others, but the reality is there is only so much we can do through technology. The human emotion of touch and caring is most times lost in text and trying to make communication easier, but it's not always easy. In fact it's hard connecting on a meaningful, one-to-one level, especially with so many people rushing to get someone's attention.

If you know the rhythms of emails in HubSpot and Salesforce, there is a human characteristic that just can't be reproduced in software or by artificial intelligence. The spirit of giving back and helping one another is at the core of what Needworking is, and we can't reproduce it exactly on a social media platform either. We can be the conduit for how people find one another and match up, but it's the power of people's passion to help someone else—the power to share knowledge you have gained on your journey and your power and ability to provide someone your knowledge, an elevator up so to speak. Actor Jack Lemmon was quoted as saying, "No matter how successful you get, always send the elevator back down."

You don't have to be a 35th-floor type of person to help someone. You might just be a step ahead but know the right people to connect with. The way we built Needworking from the ground up wasn't based on who you are connected with. It's based on having a person post a Need in the category/topic of your specialty and knowing that you can help them with your knowledge.

In chapter 4, I discussed being concise with your Need. I also feel the response and reciprocity of helping others should be thoughtful and concise as well. If you are committing to help, make sure you follow through, and if you are receiving that help, do yourself a favor and follow that through as well. Too many times I've seen responses to Needs, but the recipient just doesn't respond. Needworking only works when both parties put forth 100% commitment to the effort. If a person drops the ball on either side, that trust and potential connection is broken, and you've potentially lost a great opportunity for growth.

Also in chapter 4, I provided examples of possible Needs based on Topics. Every Need should have a concise response; here are some suggested responses to the Needs from chapter 4.

1. Accounting:

   "Certainly! I have a strong background in accounting and would be happy to assist you with your project. Please provide me with more details, and I'll do my best to help you."

2. Advertising:

   "Absolutely! I have experience in various advertising strategies and can offer guidance. Feel free to share more about your business, and I'll provide insights and recommend relevant resources to help you."

3. Banking:

    "Of course! I have a background in banking and can offer recommendations based on your new venture. Let me know your specific requirements or concerns, and I'll provide you with tips and suggestions."

4. Benefits:

    "I've been in the industry for twenty years and know employee benefits can be complex. I'd be happy to help you understand the various options available. Let's discuss your specific Needs, and I'll provide insights and answer any questions you have."

5. Employment:

    "I understand the challenges of standing out in the job market. I'd be happy to provide advice and support. Let's discuss your specific field and preferences, and I'll offer guidance and share any relevant networking connections I may have."

Please note that these answers are just somewhat general suggestions and should be tailored to the specific context and individual Needs.

Another thought leader who speaks to helping others is John Hall, the CEO of Influence & Company. In his article "10 Ways to Help Others That Will Lead You to Success,"[1] Hall emphasizes the importance of leaders helping others. Hall believes that helping

1 John Hall, "10 Ways to Help Others That Will Lead You to Success," *Forbes*, May 26, 2013, https://www.forbes.com/sites/johnhall/2013/05/26/10-ways-to-help-others-that-will-lead-you-to-success/?sh=217fae1c2bce

should be an inherent responsibility of business leaders, even though it can be challenging at times. He shares ten thoughts that serve as reminders for leaders to effectively assist others.

Hall suggests that leaders can help by sharing their knowledge and continuously educating themselves to stay ahead. Understanding what is valuable to individuals in Need of help is crucial, as it ensures the assistance provided is truly beneficial. Sharing resources and connecting people who could benefit from them is another way leaders can make a difference.

Hall also writes that leaders should be proactive in identifying and sharing opportunities that can benefit others. Providing transparent feedback and constructive criticism can help individuals improve and contribute to the success of the company. Being brand advocates, making introductions, volunteering time, recognizing others' contributions, and offering meaningful gifts during times of Need are all ways leaders can have a positive impact on those around them. By prioritizing the act of helping others, leaders can foster strong relationships and ultimately achieve success.

Finding out what people Need is getting to the heart of the matter. I don't mean to throw anyone under the bus, but I will because I tell it like it is. It's extremely frustrating to see local public leaders who get paid by our tax dollars and control money and the direction of a region not respond. Small businesses are the core of our economy, and not all small businesses want handouts from our leaders. They want to be heard and communicated with.

It has astounded me how many government decision-makers I've met who, when I circle back with them, just don't respond. I mean I know I'm not a high-powered corporate executive, but I've lived in Baltimore my whole life and have hired employees, paid my share of business taxes, and to not even get acknowledged by someone who is supported by taxpayer money is just infuriating.

It's really impressive how many executives from larger companies respond back almost immediately or within 24 hours. I was blown away when I wrote to the late Mark Butler, CEO of Ollies, and he would respond right away. It was incredible and so impressive because he was running a publicly traded company. Mark's philosophy was that of Jack Lemmon's: send the elevator back down. Mark was truly an amazing man and spent an entire day with me on the golf course when he could have been spending time with leaders of the industry or Hall of Fame baseball players during his golf tournament. Other CEOs did the same, including Lisa Rusyniak of Goodwill Industries of The Chesapeake; Mary Anne Scully, previously from Howard Bank; Calvin Butler from BGE (now at Exelon); and Bill McCarthy from Catholic Charities in Baltimore. These are true leaders in our communities, making change and helping bring their employees and local businesses together.

I realize elected officials are busy, and maybe they just had a bad day, and it wasn't just me they were avoiding. Maybe it's their inability to help solve some of the problems small businesses face because of so many bureaucratic government hurdles and so much red tape to overcome. Small businesses do so much for our community and they deserve to be heard. I would hope our future leaders are responding back to the many people who want to improve the communities around them with the technologies that are available.

"A deep sense of love and belonging is
an irreducible Need of all people. We are
biologically, cognitively, physically, and
spiritually wired to love, to be loved, and
to belong. When those Needs are not met,
we don't function as we were meant to.
We break. We fall apart. We numb. We
ache. We hurt others. We get sick."

BRENÉ BROWN

Giving back and digging deeper is what we should all be doing
in our communities, no matter the positions or titles we hold. You
could be the mayor of a city, a bricklayer, a small business owner, or
a high school student. Giving back, listening, and responding should
just come naturally, but it's difficult for many.

"To do more for the world than the world
does for you – that is success."

HENRY FORD

Listening and being responsive to someone's Needs is where it
all begins. Even if you don't have the answer you can point them in
the right direction. We will discuss this in depth in the next chapter.
I wanted to share with you some examples of strangers connecting
with others based on their Needs and topics they have selected.

Let's take an example of a recent Need someone had. This is just one example of hundreds that are already happening on the Needworking platform. Yasmin Gulamhusein posted this Need.

As her post says, she's a Georgetown student looking for interviews for grantmaking. It was a simple ask to people whom she's never met before and is not connected with. It was also concise: "I Need 15 minutes of your time." I mean, what a great question. Would you have fifteen minutes to spend with someone if you have that knowledge to share?

She marked the post with the interests of interviewing, nonprofits, and financing. Allison Anderson responded. Allison is the assistant director for The Howard County Conservancy and has a tremendous amount of knowledge.

This is as simple as it gets, and reciprocity wins! We don't know how far this connection will last in the future or what kind of ripple effect it will have on either of their networks, but it was a pretty simple engagement.

Here is another example of a Need. Whitney was looking for judges in multiple cities. What was so awesome about this was how many times this was shared (tossed) to others who could help, and the response was immediate.

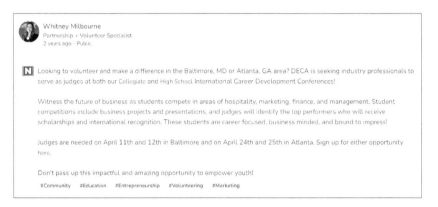

Whitney Milbourne
Partnership + Volunteer Specialist
2 years ago · Public

Looking to volunteer and make a difference in the Baltimore, MD or Atlanta, GA area? DECA is seeking industry professionals to serve as judges at both our Collegiate and High School International Career Development Conferences!

Witness the future of business as students compete in areas of hospitality, marketing, finance, and management. Student competitions include business projects and presentations, and judges will identify the top performers who will receive scholarships and international recognition. These students are career focused, business minded, and bound to impress!

Judges are needed on April 11th and 12th in Baltimore and on April 24th and 25th in Atlanta. Sign up for either opportunity here.

Don't pass up this impactful and amazing opportunity to empower youth!

#Community   #Education   #Entrepreneurship   #Volunteering   #Marketing

So you might be saying, "What's the difference between this and people asking for help on LinkedIn or Facebook?" The honest response is that there really is no difference, with the exception of connecting with people you don't know. People post Needs on LinkedIn all of the time, and they also post on Facebook and Nextdoor. People are already helping one another, when they aren't arguing on Facebook. The problem, though, is that if you have thousands of connections and the other person has thousands of connections, those Needs might get lost in the barrage of birthday posts, graduation pics, award ceremonies, news articles, sunrise pics, videos, and morning workout and animals at the office pics. People's Needs are important, and you might have missed an opportunity to sell your product or get connected because someone's pooch was in your News Feed.

Your time is valuable, and our goal with Needworking is to get you closer to helping someone else in those times of Need. The platform we have developed isn't meant to be a place where you spend hours daily.

We want to make it valuable enough that you might only have to flow in once or twice a week and make a difference for someone else, or find an Ally you can truly rely on who has a super power that you don't.

These moments of reciprocity are important and special and will help you build a trusting and lasting relationship with someone if you aren't taking advantage of them and their time. There probably isn't one networking book on the market that doesn't have a chapter dedicated to giving and helping one another. There are also books dedicated to the act of giving. In her book *The Giving Way to Happiness: Stories and Science Behind the Life-Changing Power of Giving*, author Jenny Santi explores the scientific research that provides compelling data to support the anecdotal evidence that giving is a powerful pathway to personal growth and lasting happiness. Through fMRI technology, we now know that giving activates the same parts of the brain that are stimulated by food and sex. Experiments show evidence that altruism is hardwired in the brain—and it's pleasurable. Helping others may just be the secret to living a life that is not only happier but also healthier, wealthier, more productive, and meaningful.

She also provides tips that will help you give not until it hurts, but until it feels great:

1. Find your passion
2. Give your time
3. Give to organizations with transparent aims and results
4. Find ways to integrate your interests and skills with the Needs of others
5. Be proactive, not reactive
6. Don't be guilt-tripped into giving

She makes valid points in the sense that you don't want to give just to give or gain. You shouldn't set out with the intention to gain, but you will. You want to make sure that when you give your knowledge, it has a value to someone else who can appreciate the give. Her fourth recommendation is aligned with how we set up the Needworking system with interests integrated to the skills and Needs of others.

I could go on and on about giving back and helping others; it's that important. I recall when I was in college, I was a room service waiter at the Harbor Court Hotel. We had a guest who would come every week and order the same breakfast. He was Louis Rukeyser, a renowned broadcaster on *Wall Street Week* and CNBC. I got to know Rukeyser from my morning routine of dropping off his morning juice, raspberries topped with cream, and of course, his copy of the *Wall Street Journal*. I was attending Towson at the time and wanted to get into broadcasting and was already interning at a local radio station. I had no fear of approaching him, asking myself, "What's the worst he can say?" My senior project was all things media and he allowed me to interview him at the hotel before he had to do the taping of *Wall Street Week*.

I remember sneaking the camera equipment up during my shift to make sure I didn't get fired. Rukeyser was a stutterer and some of the other staff at the hotel made fun of him, but I respected him wholeheartedly. It was amazing to watch him work because when that camera came on, that stutter disappeared.

He also provided me with a reference letter for any job in media that I was interested in. I recall going to interviews and pulling that out, and people were shocked. I didn't realize at the time what a big deal he was. It wasn't until about eight years later that PBS wanted to fire him, and it became national news and he moved over to CNBC.

I was so grateful that he provided that reference letter, and I thanked him, but I never followed up with him after I got a job in radio. I often wonder what would have occurred if I had taken the opportunity to inquire about working for him in New York City. I guess you can't keep looking back, just forward. That's why your rearview mirror is smaller than your forward windshield.

In her book *The Connector's Advantage*, Michelle Tillis Lederman states, "The key to having a generous spirit is being genuinely happy about giving. It goes hand in hand with the abundant mindset: not only do you have enough, but when you share—be it time, contacts, knowledge, or resources—you feel good about it. You're not resentful or regretful and you don't keep a scoreboard waiting for when you will be 'paid' back."

I recently spoke to the Maryland chapter of the national group 1 Million Cups (1MC). This is a free, national program designed to educate, engage, and connect entrepreneurs. Developed by the Kauffman Foundation, 1MC is based on the notion that entrepreneurs discover solutions and network over a million cups of coffee. One of the questions presented to me about Needworking was whether we should put a value on the Needs and givebacks. I understand the reasoning behind this to create a value or monetize that process, but I personally don't believe you can put a value on each giveback. Someone in your network might know a large client, and you by chance get a multimillion-dollar deal, and then there's the connected community that might help generate a deal worth a few thousand dollars. I'm just as grateful for a small opportunity as I am for a larger opportunity, as they both help keep the lights on.

Another thing I've noticed is that experienced professionals are ready, willing, and able to give their time and resources to students and people just getting started. We have had hundreds of students sign up to Needworking who are from Towson, and it just baffles me that students don't ask or post. I feel that some of these social media platforms have really hurt our society in terms of knowing how to connect with others. Just like Louis Rukeyser helped me when I was a teenager, there are millions of people who are willing to help the next generation. All you have to do is ask. If you are concerned about not knowing what to say, then just ask. I'm happy to coach you through it. Ask for an internship, ask for an opportunity, ask for a connection. Again I say, "What's the worst thing that could happen?"

You also never know who is willing to help when there's an opportunity. When I went to see how larger crowds would react to Needworking at South by Southwest (SXSW) in Austin in 2022, I didn't know what to expect. I went to see if I could get connected with investors but learned it was way too early for us. We still didn't have revenue, and we had fewer than 500 users at that point. It's definitely a steep climb when you are at the bottom of that mountain.

I wanted to figure out how Needworking fit into the landscape, and with everyone connecting on LinkedIn as the go-to platform, it's difficult to squeeze into that niche when you have a powerhouse like LinkedIn. I would go up to business leaders at the SXSW event and try to make conversation and ask questions, but they were so busy in their element that it was difficult to make inroads.

Baron Davis, former NBA player and now president of Baron Davis, was on stage along with Marshall Sandman, Hannah Bronfman from HBFIT, and Matt Rutler from MasterClass. The panel session was titled "Celebrity as Investor." I thought, *Wow, it would be amazing to get a celebrity to help us grow the audience of Needworking!* Could you imagine if celebrities were giving just one bit of feedback to members who had questions or Needed help? That would be pretty cool. Well, a magical thing happened that day. I went to speak to Baron, and as I was standing by the stage, I began talking to Tyreek Moore, who works with Baron and heads up UWish and Black Santa. Tyreek is an awesome storyteller who grew up in the Bronx and ended up going to Harvard because he believed he could. The more I heard of his story, the more I knew I had to connect him with Heart Smiles in Baltimore. It's a group that Joni Holifield created to help high school and college-age kids in Baltimore believe in themselves and help grow them into future leaders.

I asked Tyreek if he would be able to do a Zoom with the kids, and he agreed and joined us with some powerful messages that resonated with the group. He shared how he was able to grow in his career and understand his superpower. Everyone has one that sets us apart. We asked the group what they felt their superpower was, and it was incredible seeing how many people said that helping one another and empathy were the key to their success. Tyreek spoke about failure and his FADAF acronym, which stands for Failure And Difficulties Are Feedback.

I can't predict the future for these young leaders, but I hope they got something out of this event and it takes them to new heights. It was a random connection I was able to make with a complete stranger. If you don't ask, you don't know where it will go. If you are interested in watching the full interview, just head to our Needworking YouTube channel.

It was incredible to see so many young adults already want to help others as they are just learning and figuring out who they are. It reminded me of all the learning I was doing as a teenager, but I was absorbing far more to learn, and I don't think I would have put giving back as my superpower back then.

> "At the end it's not about what you have or even what you've accomplished. It's about who you've lifted up, who you've made better. It's about what you've given back."
>
> **DENZEL WASHINGTON**

The Takeaway

1. **Transcendence:** When Maslow revised his hierarchy of Needs to put transcendence above self-actualization, it suggested that once we reach a level of personal growth and self-realization, the next step is to transcend ourselves and give back to others.

2. **Benefits of giving:** Numerous studies have shown that giving back and helping others has positive effects on one's well-being. Acts of kindness, prosocial behavior, and volunteering contribute to psychological flourishing, increased life expectancy, improved immune system, reduced stress, and other health benefits.

3. **The Need for reciprocity:** Giving back should not be a one-sided effort. Reciprocity involves both parties committing to the act of helping and following through on their commitments. When trust and connection are

nurtured through reciprocal interactions, meaningful opportunities for growth and development arise.

4. **Identifying what you can give:** Everyone possesses unique gifts and abilities that can be shared with others. Sharing these gifts, no matter how big or small, can make a significant difference in someone's life.

5. **The role of technology:** While technology can facilitate connections and help people share their gifts, it cannot fully replicate the human emotion, touch, and caring that are essential in meaningful interactions. Building genuine connections and providing support both require personal engagement and effort.

6. **Leaders as agents of change:** By sharing knowledge, providing resources, offering opportunities, and fostering relationships, leaders can have a positive impact on individuals and the community. Helping should be an inherent responsibility for business leaders, as it contributes to their own success as well.

7. **Needworking as a platform for giving:** The Needworking platform exemplifies the power of reciprocal giving. Through concise and thoughtful responses to others' Needs, individuals can connect and offer their expertise, knowledge, and time. The platform serves as a conduit for people to find each other and share their gifts, fostering growth and collaboration.

8. **Overcoming barriers:** While there can be challenges in the process of giving back, it's important to make a conscious effort to prioritize helping others. Genuine

connections and community building require active engagement and open communication.

9. **Success in giving:** True success lies in doing more for the world than what the world does for you. By giving back and making a positive impact on others' lives, individuals can achieve a sense of fulfillment and contribute to the betterment of society.

Reciprocity is an important element of giving back. It encourages individuals to share their knowledge, time, and resources with others, fostering genuine connections and promoting personal and collective growth. By engaging in acts of kindness and embracing a mindset of reciprocity, you can make a difference in your own lives, and the lives of others.

CHAPTER 12

PAY IT FORWARD — THE HOT POTATO

Being a Superconnector isn't that difficult if you listen, learn, and of course connect. I can think of so many people that I have met through the years who will just point you in the right direction.

You don't Need someone to necessarily hold your hand to get to the next location of your journey. You Need Allies who might give you just five minutes at an event or a thirty-minute meeting, or introduce you to someone you should meet along the way.

Just think of your business as a new reality show. Let's call it *Networking and Alone*. You are blindfolded and dropped off in the middle of a networking event in another state and an organization you have never heard of. Let's say it's the Alaska Anthropological Association and you've worked in manufacturing your entire career. You need to power through a two hour networking challenge, figuring out what you possibly have in common and how you can help others in that room. The rules are that you cannot hide in the bathroom or a corner and must make ten meaningful connections.

The reality is you are not alone. There are millions of people who have done what you are venturing to do. The difference is you have a special quality that no one else has: you. There is only one you and you want to get others to get to know you.

People are willing to help you when you are genuine, thoughtful, and sincere in your journey. As you grow your knowledge and experience, those same people are willing to follow you on that journey. Especially if you can lead them out of the jungle and help get them to where they are going as well.

Life is a journey, and we are all heading down different roads at different times, but coming together is powerful. It reminds me of the scene in *Forrest Gump* where Forrest just decides to run, and he picks up hundreds of people along the way, just following him on that journey. He didn't do anything special; he just started a movement.

In his TED Talk "How To Start A Movement," Dereck Sivers speaks to the importance of the first follower. If you haven't seen the video of the "Lone Nut" and the first follower that Sivers includes in his talk, it's a must watch. To summarize, a man is at a concert dancing all over the place, and people are just staring and making judgments about this "lone nut." That is, until someone joins him in his arms-flailing motion, and then you see dozens of people join the process.

Just like Forrest Gump, this Lone Nut didn't get to know these individuals on a deeper level, but for that moment in time they were all connected in his running cohort. It's up to you to find those connections that matter, but get people involved in what you are doing by being the first follower of someone else. Volunteer at an event or help someone raise money for a charity, for example.

You can help others along the way. No matter your age or your work experience, you have Allies and Trusted Allies who you know that you can share information with. If someone Needs directions and guidance on their journey, pay it forward and help them out. This doesn't have to be a reciprocal action at this very moment. It can be an action that you put out in the world, and karma will always prevail. You will get that back in return someday.

One of the surprise recent reads for me was Jay Shetty's *Think Like a Monk*. Going through my own inner emotional turmoil after my father passed in 2020, I saw the book in the airport and thought, *I Need inner peace and to get my mind in a different place.* Little did I know that the book was going to be filled with chapters about connecting and surrounding yourself with the people who matter the most and have their most thoughtful intentions for you. There is so much I could highlight from this book, but I highly recommend you read it for yourself.

In one chapter, Shetty has an illustration of a "circle of love." He writes, "Our lack of gratitude is what makes us feel unloved. When we think nobody cares we NEED to check ourselves and realize that the love we give out comes back in a variety of sources, whatever we put out will come back to us." This is an example of karma; the idea that your actions, good or bad, bring the same back to you. When we feel unloved, we Need to ask ourselves: Am I offering help as often as I ask for help? Who is giving to me without receiving anything in return?

On social media, people share funny stories or opportunities that exist with others. The Needworking version of sharing is something we like to call a Hot Potato. You might recall sitting in a circle in elementary school to play the hot potato game. You pretended the potato was on fire, and you had to get it out of your hands quicker than anyone else and over to the next person without dropping it.

Now, just think about someone's journey. To them it's important at that moment in time. I've seen LinkedIn messages come into my inbox asking for help, and I've completely missed them because of the spam sales pitches. I honestly feel horrible when I miss an opportunity to help someone or someone they are connected to. I feel like I dropped a Hot Potato and I let that person and their Ally down.

The reason we set up Needworking the way we did was to ensure that you are getting alerted in your Need Feed in a category that you specialize in. This puts a Need right at the top of the importance pile. The way algorithms work now on social media, you might miss something that you could have been an integral part of, and you could have been a guide to someone in their journey.

As I mentioned in chapter 11 about reciprocity, it's healthy and refreshing to be able to help someone, and you've missed the opportunity to do so because the ask got lost among posts about vacations or pictures of their canine office sidekick. Our social feeds tend to get cluttered, and we miss opportunities with so much noise. We don't have that much time in the day, much less life, and we should be able to use every minute of it to move forward in our journeys and bring someone else along at the same time.

How a Hot Potato works on Needworking is that you simply share that Need with others you know or are connected to. (Hence the importance of building your Allies and Trusted Allies on the platform.) I've tried to tag people on LinkedIn and forward them an opportunity, and again it's amazing to me how little time people have for others. You Need to be smart, thoughtful, and patient with those you are paying it forward to. Some people just may not see the world the same way you do as a giver, and your philosophies will never meet. That being said, if you do happen to send them a Hot Potato and they don't respond and you see them at an event, just ask and follow up.

I know I keep bringing up Brené Brown, but in her book *Rising Strong*, she talks about what people are going through at different moments. You might have something that is absolutely a high priority or a Hot Potato, and the person you share it with ignores you. You can't let it eat away at you. You don't know what that person is going through—they could be in crisis or just unaware of your Needs and feelings based on their own circumstances. It's all about timing. Sending a Hot Potato isn't perfect, but the rewards will come back to you if you send enough and are willing to help others, who in turn will be willing to help you.

So, we recently had fun creating a unique Hot Potato graphic. Ladies and gentlemen as well as my nonbinary friends, I must apologize in advance. Your face plastered on a round potbelly potato probably isn't the best look, but our designers were just having fun with the concept.

We wanted to have fun with it because, well honestly, it's a childhood game and we can't always be uber-serious about business. We should have some things that will break the mundane. It's no different from WeWork adding beer pong to their happy hours. Some people will appreciate it and enjoy the creativeness of a Hot Potato, while others will just avoid it.

Now you have plenty of opportunities to send a Hot Potato with our system. I recently showcased Needworking at a start-up event, and I put potatoes all around the display table. It confused the hell out of people, but they loved it once I explained. The Carberry lineage is Irish Catholic. and my great-grandparents came to the United

States from Ireland in 1912. Needworking's color is kelly green, and it's a tribute to my family's Irish heritage. You probably know where I'm going with this, but there will be no Irish Potato Famine with Needworking.

We are encouraging our users to pay it forward and share the Needs of others. We have designed the platform so that you can not only share a Hot Potato in Needworking with people you know, but you can also send that opportunity to a connection or followers on other platforms like Facebook, Twitter, and LinkedIn, or just copy the link and use it in Slack or internal company communications.

Needworking is also counting those Potatoes that are being sent. Since Hot Potato was inspired by a game, each month we are going to be counting how many Potatoes are being tossed in our Hot Potato Challenge. Years ago you could become the King of Foursquare, if you remember that check-in app. We have borrowed some of the fun ideas of days past and rolled them into our own way to have fun connecting with people. We know business is serious, but you don't have to take yourself too seriously all the time. Hopefully, we'll see your name on the leader board or as the Hot Potato Champion of the month.

The Takeaway

Being a Superconnector is about listening, learning, and connecting with others. By offering genuine help and support, you can build valuable connections and create a powerful network.

Superconnectors can pay it forward through the Hot Potato approach on Needworking, which allows participants to share opportunities and help others. It's important to form genuine connections and help others on their journey.

Being a "first follower" is important as it can initiate a chain reaction of support.

Surround yourself with people who have thoughtful intentions, and build Allies and Trusted Allies.

Use patience and understanding when reaching out to others, taking into consideration their circumstances and priorities.

Becoming a Superconnector and paying it forward allows you to build a strong network, assist others on their journey, and ultimately receive support in return.

CHAPTER 13

THE 48-HOUR RULE

W hat's the 48-Hour Rule? It's pretty simple: reconnect with people you met at a networking event within a 48-hour time frame after meeting them. It's that simple.

I know, you're right; it's not that simple, but you have to create your own strategies by reconnecting with those you met who you feel could have an impact on your goals and what you aim to achieve. The key is the 48 hours. If you don't act within the 48 hours, you will get busy planning another networking event and just not reach out to someone who might have been a great Ally.

Systems and processes are extremely important, and it's up to you to design the best way to connect with those who can provide the knowledge you are seeking, an account you'd like to work with, or a future company you would like to work for.

Why do I term it the 48-Hour Rule? I impose that rule on myself, and oftentimes I don't follow my own timelines. As I was putting together this chapter based on what I would do, I figured

I might as well get input from others to see if my thinking was on target or flawed.

The first thing I did was go to LinkedIn and create a poll. If you haven't created a poll, I would highly recommend trying it out. It's one of that platform's best features. The only problem I have with it is how people use it. I really don't care if you are going to watch the Superbowl or what your favorite music genre is. People put up the most ridiculous polls to clutter your feed. I prefer targeted business polls.

Here is the poll I put up for the 48-Hour Rule:

How quickly *should you* (not *do you*) follow up with someone after meeting them at a Networking event?

Right after the event ended	7%
Within 24 hours	43%
Within 48 hours	36%
Within 72 hours	14%

56 votes · Poll closed

As you can see 86% of the respondents came back and said within 48 hours. It wasn't a huge sample size, but enough to know that I was headed in the right direction.

The second research tactic was putting it on Needworking. com, of course. I posed that question regarding how people follow up, and a couple admitted that they are absolutely horrible at it: https://www.Needworking.com/post/63a073810ecc48f78fa6c70d

Colleen McKenna from Intero Advisory stated that she follows up within 24-48 hours: "Personalized connection request on LinkedIn, follow-up message acknowledging the connection and, if appropriate, next steps—move to email and even phone!"

McKenna is a LinkedIn expert, and I highly recommend her book *It's Business, Not Social.* She has been working with companies all over the US and helping their employees put some of those actions in place, from cleaning up their LinkedIn profiles to the way to connect with others.

The one common theme that many of the people I interview agree on is making that connection through LinkedIn. I agree with them that it's easy to do and a necessary part of the process. The big problem, though, is the noise and staying focused. You must research and develop your own process of connecting with people versus just hitting that "connect" button.

McKenna says, "Collecting a business card has little context without following up. Connecting on LinkedIn with a particular person of interest/strategic connection that can be a potential lead, client, employer, or investor places you in their network. The benefit: it strengthens your network, shows you others that are similar, your mutual points of connection at their company. It also leads to gleaning others in their company that may be part of a buying community or can help you make a stronger connection or provide access. Way more valuable than one business card with one name on it."

Use tools that get you closer to a connection with someone. McKenna recommends you take the time to use LinkedIn Sales Navigator. You can also take the conversation simply to email or a phone call, or get more extensive like adding them to Needworking or funnel resources like HubSpot, Pipedrive, Salesforce, or whatever CRM system you use in your process. The difference is that you can have a small group of people to communicate with and create Allies and not get overwhelmed.

What it comes down to is your process and how you want to connect with someone you just met. If you walked away from a networking event with fifteen to twenty cards, are you really going to reconnect with all of them or choose a select few?

Jill Porter from Anne Arundel County Economic Development added, "I typically follow up with a personalized LinkedIn message right after the networking engagement (or within 24 hours at latest) and I try to remember something specific about them to bring up. If they are a lead I want to build a relationship with, I mention that I'll be emailing them (and a time frame to expect it to be received) so that if it gets stuck in spam they are more likely to look out for it and find it. I then email to gain their availability and schedule either a virtual or face-to-face discussion, based on the synergy and specifics of the conversation I'd like to cultivate. If I don't gain a response from either means of communication within a day or two, I'll call to make sure it was received and scheduled over the phone."

Chad Bolen from the Baltimore Orioles also jumped in and recommended that writing a handwritten note is still one of the best attention-getters.

It's best to follow up with someone you just met at a networking event within one to two days after the event. This shows that you value their time and are interested in maintaining the relationship. Here's a general guideline for following up:

1. Send a personalized email or message thanking the person for their time and reiterating the key points of your conversation.

2. Mention any relevant information you promised to share, such as an article or connection.

3. Ask if it would be okay to keep in touch in the future and if they would like to schedule a call or meeting.

4. End the message by reiterating your appreciation for the person's time and expertise.

Remember to keep the follow-up brief, friendly, and professional, and to respect the other person's time and preferences. If they don't respond or if they decline to connect further, don't take it personally, and move on to the next networking opportunity.

The Process

When you are at one of the numerous networking events we described in previous chapters, ask for the best way to reconnect with the person you're talking to. Always remember to engage and listen. When you aren't engaged in a conversation, people will know and sense it. They also might not respond to you on LinkedIn when you try to reach out later. Listen and engage and get some form of contact data, whether it's a card, a QR code scan, or simply taking a photo of their card or name badge.

Remember the story of that fly hitting the window back in chapter 8? Do something different if your process isn't working. Are you asking new contacts what you can help them with? Come up with a great question that will get them to remember you especially for being so thoughtful.

Try questions like these:

➤ If there was one thing that I could help you with in the next week or so, what would that be?

➤ Who is your ideal client or customer, and how can I help you utilize my network?

Questions like these do several things:

1. They show you are interested in them and you'd like to reconnect with them.
2. They give you a timeline in which you Need to act.
3. If they are willing to tell you at that moment, you will get to know someone more deeply in that room compared to what others are doing.
4. If you can't help them, you might know of someone whom you can connect them with.

I know it can be extremely disappointing when someone doesn't reach out to you after they say they will. Here's the story of one of my experiences with that. I went to a media event in Washington, DC, where we had the opportunity to present Needworking. The host of the event, Paul Duning from Capital Communicator, puts on an awesome advertising and communications show every year. The content and speakers are always top-notch. Paul had seen the work we had been doing on Needworking from the start, and he had watched us grow and knew we weren't making any revenue. It's special when someone recognizes what you are doing and wants to get involved and learn more.

I was in one of the sessions, and a younger group of business professionals was discussing what they Need to broaden their careers.

Down the line, each and every one of them said networking and con-necting with people that would fit in their circles. Networking was the primary tactic for their advancement and growth.

One person on the panel was talking about almost all of the prin-ciples I go out and discuss with others. It gave me goosebumps that someone twenty years younger than me could see the things I have seen and understand the full value of their network. I speak to a lot of college kids, and half the time I feel the glazed stare and wonder what they are thinking.

I went up to this person after the panel and told her all about my Needworking project. She seemed excited, asked for my card, and said, "I will reach out to you within 48 hours." I almost had to sit down. Wow, are you kidding me? Someone actually put a task on themselves to make a deeper connection. It was truly hard to believe. Very cool!

Needless to say, that 48-hour window passed, and I never heard back. She did sign into the platform and I tried to connect, but she didn't respond.

Why did I want to connect with her in the first place? To be honest, it was to see how we can find those people just like her who are willing to connect on a different level. I wanted to find out how I get the twenty-somethings in conversations with people in their thirties and forties or older and see if they can all share knowledge that we all can learn from. I know twenty-somethings are communicating and making things happen, I just don't know how and what tools they are typically using.

Now here's the thing about networking. You can't be too hard on yourself when someone doesn't reach back out or take action. It's really not something that interests them, or it's bad timing. I know during the two years I dealt with losing my parents I had a tough time focusing, and life isn't easy and people have their own agendas. Maybe it was because the conference was held in the beginning of November and you're in the middle of Q4 closing out the year and then the holidays hit. Who knows? Take a step back and try to regroup again in January. If there is radio silence, then it wasn't meant to be.

At conferences I do my best to take pictures of the speakers or screenshot the agenda to get their information to reach back out.

One of the tactics I have used that works extremely well is to ask for a virtual meeting as a follow-up. If you met someone and it was brief and you didn't exactly have a strong enough connection to grab a cup of coffee in person, just do an online call. I'd recommend using a calendar invite tool like Calendly, HubSpot, or Pipedrive. I have created a template to make sure I add the person's data in my CRM, and it inserts a few items I've set on the template like name, business, and website. The email works a majority of the time.

Here's a sample of the message I use. Adapt as you see fit for your own networking:

Dear _____

It was so nice to meet you at the ACG Richmond event. I really appreciate the time you took to help me navigate the meeting and make some new connections. I'd like to take some time to reconnect and learn more about _____Business Name_____ and who your ideal client/customer is and how I can help you connect with others in my network.

Here's my calendar access. I would love to jump on a quick meet and greet when you have time—book some time here.

*In the meantime I'll jump on _____ website_____
and learn more.*

Sincerely,
Dave

Reconnecting is a trial-and-error occurrence. I've had my fair share of rejection and no response to messages I've sent. Whenever I get rejected, I think of the famous words by coach Jim Valvano, who died way before his time: "Never give up! Failure and rejection are only the first step to succeeding."

The Takeaway

The 48-Hour Rule emphasizes the importance of reconnecting with people you meet at networking events within 48 hours. This rule serves as a guideline to ensure timely follow-up and maintain valuable connections.

To effectively implement the 48-Hour Rule, design your own strategies for reconnecting based on your goals and objectives. Take the initiative to ask for the best way to reconnect with individuals and engage in meaningful conversations to gather relevant contact information.

LinkedIn is a valuable platform for reconnecting, but it's crucial to navigate through the noise and stay focused on your objectives. Personalized connection requests and follow-up messages on LinkedIn strengthen relationships and help you demonstrate genuine interest in others.

Using additional tools like Needworking, LinkedIn Sales Navigator, email, phone calls, or CRM systems can enhance your networking efforts and manage connections effectively. These tools provide a means to connect on a deeper level, offer assistance, and schedule further discussions or meetings.

When reconnecting, ask thoughtful questions that show your interest in the other person and offer assistance. This approach not only deepens the connection but also provides an opportunity to learn and potentially make valuable introductions.

While the 48-Hour Rule is essential, it's important not to be too hard on yourself if someone doesn't respond or take action. Life circumstances or timing may affect their responsiveness. Be patient and try again if there's no response, but ultimately, if there's consistent radio silence, it may not be meant to be.

As you reconnect, consider asking for virtual meetings if a strong connection for a coffee meeting isn't established. Using calendar invitation tools like Calendly, HubSpot, or Pipedrive can streamline the scheduling process and increase the likelihood of successful meetings.

Reconnecting is a trial-and-error process, and not every attempt will result in a positive response. Embrace failures and rejections as stepping stones to success, and never give up on building valuable connections.

Remember, the 48-Hour Rule is a guideline, and the key is to take timely action to nurture relationships and leverage the potential opportunities that networking events present.

CHAPTER 14

GET BACK TO CONVERSATION AND CUT THE FAT

As social media transitions to more viewable content and the "Follow Me" culture, I sometimes wonder if conversations with top-level celebrities are really even possible on social media platforms. When you are putting posts up on social media, are they just to get attention and increase followers? Will AI take these celebrities and morph them into an interactive advisor like Marlon Brando's character was in *Superman*?

How often do you get in a conversation with Kim Kardashian or Howard Stern? You typically don't. When I worked in radio at the Howard Stern station, I was lucky enough to have had a couple of conversations with Howard Stern, but this just doesn't happen normally.

For decades, radio and television were the mediums that were the primary connectors to what was happening in the world. It was a one-to-many relationship. The telephone and face-to-face interaction were where one-to-one conversations were happening. That model got turned on its head when the internet came along. The opportunity to have conversations in a more intimate setting is here now, and people are getting paid for their interactions.

Let's take a look at an app like Cameo. You pay to have a celebrity leave a personal message for a friend or loved one, or even promote a business. I have purchased several Cameos, and they are just awesome. You might not have a personal relationship with a celebrity, but you feel a little more connected than just seeing them on TV. Technology is constantly changing, and Cameo was smart enough to add longer forms of connecting if the personality is willing to do it. You and your family or friends could have a call with them and interact on a personal level. The Baltimore Ravens do this for season ticket holders. They will host a player conversation, and a selected group can participate in the live stream event. Where once before it was one to millions, now it can be one to clusters.

The thought of taking what was thought to be an untouchable experience has actually become more of reality, and with a little money and a little luck, you can make these experiences happen. You don't typically expect any deep conversations out of this, but the experience nonetheless is pretty cool.

Now let's look at someone you have had one-to-one conversations with and know personally. The advent of social media has changed the way we act and communicate. The larger the following they get, the more they broadcast and try to put their messages out to the masses and lose all sense of personalization. I have to admit that I am guilty of this. I have put things out there in the hopes of reaching larger groups and connecting with others, and it has been both a success and a failure. You have to know your audience, and there is a methodology as to whom you tag and what's advantageous for getting awareness.

I have to say, the older I get, the older that style of communication gets. I just want to be with my people, and it gives me a greater appreciation of those twenty-somethings who don't really Need to connect with me.

It's not just social media, but it's also my inbox. I get flooded with hundreds of emails every day, and I get notifications of events that people want me to attend. I often respond with a follow-up email that thanks the sender for the invitation and lets them know I'll take a look at my calendar and see what my schedule looks like that week.

Since they have taken my time to try and sell me on something they are doing, I feel it's only reciprocal to offer something I'm doing as well. I will let them know that they can also list their event on Need-working.com to generate additional attendees and awareness. I look at this as a win-win for them. It's free and will only take ten to fifteen minutes of their time and possibly get their event noticed by hundreds of other people who could benefit from attending their event.

It's disappointing to me that people don't respond in this situation, and they have the opportunity to get their event noticed by a new audience. I realize you are working to sell your services, and you've cluttered my inbox with messages that I take the time to read and respond, and you don't offer the same courtesy. The same goes with the lack of response on social media platforms and your Instant Message notifications.

How much time have you wasted when someone isn't reciprocal and is only looking out for themselves?

CUT THE FAT!

By that I mean, get rid of what's unnecessary or superfluous.

Why are you allowing these people to infiltrate your LinkedIn feed or inbox if they aren't willing to help you in return? It's like the car dealer that puts the advertising wrap around your license plate. Do you know how many cars you've advertised their dealership to, and what did you get for that in return? At least give me free oil changes for promoting your company. Reciprocity in relationships matters. If you are not getting the same respect you are giving, cut the fat!

Take the time to go to your unresponsive connections and unsubscribe from their emails and unfollow and remove them as a connection. It's okay to stop reading and do it now. I'll wait. I'll run downstairs to make another cup of coffee while you are doing that.

I feel so much satisfaction after washing them away. Now you might bump into them at a networking event, or they might try to reconnect. If this happens, you simply Need to be honest and let them know that your time and network are important to you. You would rather commit the time to the people that are more receiving of your advice and knowledge. One man's trash is another man's treasure.

You want to have deeper conversations with those who treasure and value you.

"The less of these you have,
the more one is worth."

THE JOKER TO THE RIDDLER IN *THE BATMAN* (2022)

THE ANSWER: A FRIEND.

I recall Madonna using the acronym GROI: Get Rid Of It if you don't Need it.

Spend time with the people who matter. Here is a list of twenty-five ways to set guidelines for improving how you are decluttering your social feeds and utilizing Needworking principles:

1. **Evaluate your current contacts:** Assess your existing contact list, keeping in mind Dunbar's number and Maslow's hierarchy. Focus on maintaining relationships that fulfill your social Needs and contribute to your personal growth.

2. **Prioritize close relationships:** Nurture connections with close friends and family members, supporting each other's Needs and aspirations.

3. **Consider Dunbar's layers:** Allocate time and energy to the innermost layer of close relationships while recognizing the varying levels of connection in your network.

4. **Identify acquaintances:** Gradually reduce contacts with acquaintances who do not contribute significantly to your well-being, allowing you to focus on those who matter most.

5. **Streamline your friend lists:** Unfriend or unfollow individuals with whom you no longer feel a strong connection or whose values and interests no longer align with yours.

6. **Limit networking connections:** Be selective when expanding your professional network, focusing on individuals who can help fulfill your career Needs and vice versa.

7. **Optimize privacy settings:** Adjust privacy settings to control the visibility of your profile and posts, ensuring you share personal content only with trusted connections.

8. **Utilize lists or groups:** Organize contacts based on shared interests or relationships, facilitating targeted interactions, and reducing noise in your feed.

9. **Mute or hide irrelevant content:** Use features to mute or hide content from contacts whose updates are irrelevant to your Needs and goals.

10. **Curate your newsfeed:** Follow accounts that provide valuable content aligned with your aspirations while unfollowing or muting accounts that distract you from your Big Rocks.

11. **Limit new connection requests:** Accept new connections that align with your desired network size and goals, focusing on quality over quantity.

12. **Practice digital decluttering:** Regularly review your contacts, decluttering and refocusing your network to match your evolving Needs.

13. **Engage in offline interactions:** Invest time in building and maintaining offline relationships, which often have a more significant impact on your well-being.

14. **Embrace quality over quantity:** Prioritize deep, meaningful connections over a large number of superficial connections, helping you fulfill higher-order Needs.

15. **Consider Maslow's hierarchy of Needs:** Reflect on your social connections in the context of that hierarchy, ensuring they contribute to your sense of belonging, love, and self-actualization.

16. **Seek supportive relationships:** Surround yourself with individuals who support your Needs and aspirations, and reciprocate by helping them fulfill their Needs as well.

17. **Regularly reassess your network:** Continuously evaluate your social network, ensuring it aligns with your changing Needs, goals, and desire for personal growth.

18. **Practice active listening:** Engage in conversations by actively listening and understanding the Needs of your contacts, offering support and assistance when possible.

19. **Limit time spent on social media:** Allocate specific periods for social media usage, ensuring it does not impede your ability to tackle your Big Rocks and support others in meeting their Needs.

20. **Cultivate offline hobbies and interests:** Build your Mountain List of offline activities and interests, balancing your social media usage with fulfilling experiences outside the digital realm.

21. **Be authentic:** Show authenticity in your online interactions, building trust and fostering connections based on shared values and Needs.

22. **Set boundaries:** Establish clear boundaries for social media usage, allowing time for personal growth, supporting others, and tackling your Big Rocks without excessive distractions.

23. **Practice empathy:** Show empathy and understanding toward your contacts, acknowledging their Needs and supporting them in their journeys.

24. **Foster diversity:** Seek connections with individuals from diverse backgrounds and perspectives, broadening your understanding of others' Needs and fostering a richer social network.

25. **Focus on personal growth:** Utilize social media as a tool for personal growth by following accounts that provide valuable

insights, ideas, and inspiration, supporting you in fulfilling your Needs and achieving your goals.

By integrating principles from Dunbar's number and Maslow's hierarchy of Needs, building your Mountain List, and tackling your Big Rocks, you can create a clutter-free social media experience that fosters personal growth, meaningful connections, and overall well-being.

I know I have mentioned this previously, but I would also recommend reading or listening to Steven's Covey's *First Things First* and *Seven Habits of Highly Effective People*.

On a personal note, I recently attended a funeral for the mother of a friend of mine. He spoke about his mom and what he had learned, and it was one of the best and most cherished lists I have ever heard. This list is not only personal but relates so much to business. I'm sharing it with you, courtesy of Dan and his late mom, Kathie Taylor:

1. Wake up early. Get stuff done while everyone else is still sleeping.
2. Dress sharp. You can never be overdressed for any occasion.
3. Keep your house neat—like a freshly cleaned hotel room neat.
4. Make lists and cross things off of them as you go.
5. Keep a calendar; and keep it full of events and fun stuff.
6. Always be on time.
7. Never forget a birthday or anniversary of the people you care about.
8. Say "yes" to every invitation. Figure out a way to be there.
9. Always be more interested in what the other person is saying vs. talking about yourself.
10. Be reliable. Always do what you say you're going to do, when you said you'd do it.

11. Take lots of pictures to capture memories as they happen.
12. Work hard, and make friends at work.
13. Family is everything. Stay close and stay in touch.
14. Travel often and explore the world.
15. And finally, make lifelong friendships, and fight like hell to keep them.

Just like building your Mountain Lists, creating a values list like this one is incredible. Dan and his entire family have been guided in this way with his mom's principles. Making lifelong friendships and fighting like hell to keep them rings incredibly true, especially in difficult times. Just know that it's okay to eliminate people from your circle of influence. If the conversations they are having are one-sided, it's time to move on and find other friends who will engage with you the way you deserve to be treated.

The Takeaway

There are huge benefits to social media, but there's also an incredible downside, where personalization and meaningful connections are often lost in the pursuit of attention and follower counts. We may share our own experiences of reaching out to people on platforms like LinkedIn and email, only to be met with silence or a lack of reciprocity. This lack of response can be frustrating and time-wasting.

To address this issue, eliminate unnecessary connections and declutter your social media feeds and inboxes. Prioritize meaningful relationships, unfollow or unfriend individuals who no longer contribute significantly to your well-being, and set guidelines for improving your social media experience.

It's a blessing to spend time with people who value and appreciate your presence. Authentic conversations, personal growth, and empathy in building meaningful connections is the key.

Be aware of the changing nature of conversations in the age of social media, the value of personalization, and the Need to eliminate people from your social platforms who do not reciprocate meaningful interactions. By focusing on quality over quantity and fostering connections that contribute to personal growth and well-being, you can create a clutter-free social media experience that nurtures deep connections and authentic conversations.

CHAPTER 15

PULL IT ALL TOGETHER WITH YOUR INSIGHT AND EXPERTISE

I predict that in the next five to ten years, artificial intelligence (AI) will dominate the way we gather data and start communicating. Our thoughts and ideas will be filled with the knowledge base of what web crawlers and scrapers are pulling off the internet, and it will bleed into our In Real Life (IRL) experiences.

Whatever technologies come about, we will still have Needs, and they won't be controlled by artificial intelligence. Those Needs are from the intelligence and beautiful human minds each and every one of us has.

No matter your occupation, your social platforms, your religious and cultural beliefs, your relationships, and your Need for alone time, you will have Needs that are your own. Artificial intelligence can't replace that human connectivity.

Your expertise and experiences are something worth telling and sharing. It's a knowledge base for others to learn from. A great quote from Jay Shetty's *Think Like a Monk* that resonated with me was, "Plant trees under whose shade you do not plan to sit." This book and the Needworking platform are my trees, so to speak. I've enjoyed helping connect so many people to one another over the years. I felt the Need to share my learnings and processes of my journey.

Assisting individuals, whether at a personal level or through community-based projects designed for the benefit of future generations, embodies the concept of leaving a meaningful legacy. Our capacity to learn and generously share information holds the potential to profoundly influence others. This legacy of positive impact becomes a narrative we can proudly share with others, emphasizing the enduring value of collaborative efforts and knowledge dissemination.

On Needworking, we recently launched our Insights feature, which isn't you asking someone for help. Instead, it's you providing searchable content for others to come and read based on the Topics that are covered. We felt that we wanted to include a way for users to share long-form articles and plant a tree for others to enjoy.

In their book *The Power of Giving*, Azim Jamal and Harvey McKinnon speak to giving back your knowledge: "Everyone (yes everyone) has a story to tell, and experience that can help others. Your challenge is to extract these gems from your brain and your heart and, if you can, share them with others. When you share your knowledge with others you break down barriers. You build openness and trust. By sharing knowledge, you become more valuable to your social networks and to the people you meet."

Needworking's Insights feature emphasizes the profound benefits of service in connecting and empowering individuals. Engaging in the distribution of your knowledge is providing service to others. Loneliness becomes a rare experience as the act of serving others brings people together. Through service, our gratitude is amplified, expanding our perspective on the abundance we possess. Serving others provides a holistic view of all that we have and fosters appreciation for the blessings in our lives.

Moreover, service cultivates compassion within us. By actively serving, we become aware of the world's Needs and recognize the value of what we have to offer. Witnessing the impact we can make through our service further deepens our empathy for others.

A significant outcome of service is the development of self-esteem. When we assist others, they affirm that our actions are making a difference in the world. This affirmation instills a sense of meaning and purpose within us, reinforcing our belief that we are capable of positively impacting others' lives.

In Needworking's Insights feature, service to others occupies the top tier of Maslow's hierarchy, transcending self-actualization. It highlights the reciprocal nature of service, where the act of helping others not only fulfills their Needs but also satisfies our own desire for self-fulfillment and transcendence.

One of the reasons I created Needworking was because of the anger and hate on social media platforms. In 2020, not only did we see the rise of a horrible virus that took lives from millions but it also took our humanity. Social media was disgusting. If you were on a blue side, a red side, a white side, a black side, a mask side, or just in it for me, people were horrible to one another. As I was dealing with the pain of losing my father, there were so many people posting that this virus wasn't as fatal as pneumonia. George Floyd was murdered, and riots were breaking out all over cities. It was one of the worst times on our planet, and the people on social media were vicious. It's one of the factors that led to me developing a platform where people could use the internet for good and help one another, instead of a verbal beatdown.

A Pew Research Center study done in July 2020 found that "about two-thirds of Americans (64%) say social media have a mostly negative effect on the way things are going in the country today. Just one in ten Americans say social media sites have a mostly positive effect on the way things are going, and one-quarter say these platforms have a neither positive nor negative effect."

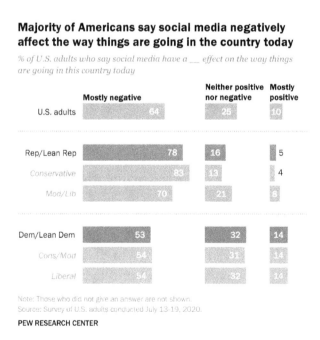

Majority of Americans say social media negatively affect the way things are going in the country today

% of U.S. adults who say social media have a ___ effect on the way things are going in this country today

	Mostly negative	Neither positive nor negative	Mostly positive
U.S. adults	64	25	10
Rep/Lean Rep	78	16	5
Conservative	83	13	4
Mod/Lib	70	21	8
Dem/Lean Dem	53	32	14
Cons/Mod	54	31	14
Liberal	54	32	14

Note: Those who did not give an answer are not shown.
Source: Survey of U.S. adults conducted July 13-19, 2020.

PEW RESEARCH CENTER

The researchers added: "When asked to elaborate on the main reason why they think social media have a mostly negative effect on the way things are going in this country today, roughly three-in-ten (28%) respondents who hold that view mention the spreading of misinformation and made-up news. Smaller shares reference examples of hate, harassment, conflict and extremism (16%) as a main reason, and 11% mention a perceived lack of critical thinking skills among many users—voicing concern about people who use these sites believing everything they see or read or being unsure about what to believe."[2]

In that environment, I found I wanted to create a social media platform that was meant to bring people together on a Need level and not just a "Look at Me" level.

From start to finish, here is how I see our Needworking System helps benefit you on your journey of self or to connect with and help others:

1. **Start with your Mountain List.** Every thirty days at a minimum, concentrate on your Apex Goal and the Big Rocks and who along the way can help you with these goals.

2. **Pick and choose your Topics.** What Topics do you want to engage in with others? We are ever changing and therefore your interests and Topics can change based on your current situational Needs.

3. **Dig deep into what you Need and why.** If you have a Need, let others know about it, and don't be afraid to ask. Be concise. If you are taking the time to ask for something, make it count and know what you Need.

4. **Shift your networking into G.E.A.R.** and plan out your strategy.

5. **Find good groups to belong to** that are either in your community/locale, faith-based, an association that is Topic-based, a sports league, or something that moves you forward towards your goals.

6. **Pick and find events that encompass what you are trying to achieve**, whether it's learning, presenting, connecting, or selling. Topical events are a strategic way to connect and find others with similar interests and Needs.

7. **Utilize the Dunbar's number theory** and build your Allies and Trusted Allies. If you aren't a social media creator and deem yourself a connector, find the right connections that matter most to achieve your success.

8. **Be inclusive and open in who your Allies are.** Don't just build your Allies from people you grew up or went to school with. Pick up new, diverse connections along the way and cut ties with those who aren't adding value to your journey.

9. **Reciprocity and referrals.** While you're gaining and achieving, you should also be giving and helping others along the way. Don't just have friends; create fans because you help connect, refer, and provide insights that others don't.

10. **If you can't fulfill a Need, Hot Potato it to someone who can.** Doing so shows your level of reciprocity and thoughtfulness.

11. **Write an Insight and share your knowledge with others on the Needworking platform.** People are searching for topics, and if you are a specialist in your field, it could be a potential connection or lead for you.

12. **Remember the 48-Hour Rule** and respond to people you have just connected with recently.

13. **Enjoy the journey.** There will be rough patches and bumps along the way, but you can learn from the distances you travel, the rocks and mountains you climb, and the apexes you reach.

14. **Ask.** What's the worst thing that can happen if you ask?

Creating Needworking is by far the greatest challenge I've had and yet the most rewarding. Technology has done incredible things by bringing us together. Years ago, you wouldn't have known what most of your high school friends were doing; now, you can easily find out through platforms like Facebook.

As technology grows, so should our own insights—insights on how we can help one another, insights on the knowledge you have that others may seek.

It's times like these that we should be coming together as a community and not tearing each other down based on our beliefs. At times, media and technology can drive a wedge between us as humans. You now have so many voices sharing their opinions that traditional media is sometimes struggling to provide objective reporting.

I'd like to see a world that is coming together and using social media as a tool that promotes the spirit of what we are as we come together.

I know it's idealistic, but I think back to when I was kid and that Coca Cola commercial came on. People of all nationalities, colors, and ages joined together on a hilltop singing in perfect harmony.[3]

That's just one song that plays in my head as I think of the Needworking process. The other is "Lean on Me." I feel it's the perfect music bed for a Needworking Superbowl commercial.

3 Coca-Cola commercial, 1971, https://www.youtube.com/watch?v=ib-Qiyklq-Q

I realize we all are not going to be in perfect harmony, but just because you see a post on social media doesn't mean you have to react with hatred to another human being. We Need to be at peace with one another. It's okay to say let's agree that we disagree, but the evil that comes out isn't Needed.

We are merely human and we aren't meant to be alone. We also aren't miracle workers, but we all can be Needworkers, helping one another strive to be the very best for one another. You never know how your help will impact another person. Something that might be small to you may become a miracle for someone else.

> "Just as treasures are uncovered from the earth, so virtue appears from good deeds, and wisdom appears from a pure and peaceful mind. To walk safely through the maze of human life, one Needs the light of wisdom and the guidance of virtue."
>
> **BUDDHA**

Take the time to use our Needworking platform to help someone fulfill a Need. Share Needworking with a friend or two. I understand that your days are busy and you might not be able to spend hours and hours on it, but spend thirty minutes a week on Needworking. Maybe set it in your calendar and plan it out. As our audience grows and more requests are posted, you might find yourself spending more time than you expected on it. I know I do. Finally, if you have a Need or a question, be vulnerable, be concise, and please don't hesitate to reach out to me. Just ask me what your Need is and feel free to message me on my profile page.

CHAPTER 16

THE NEEDWORKING PLATFORM OVERVIEW

T his book wasn't meant to be a platform instruction manual, but rather a deep dive into why I feel the Needworking System should be a viable way to connect and a better way to network. If someone wants to write the *Needworking for Dummies* book, I can collaborate with you, but it's not on my Mountain List.

I do feel that individuals will take pieces of what I have developed and create what's best for them. We learn from each other, and Needworking wouldn't have been possible without the wisdom of Abraham Maslow, Robin Dunbar, Dale Carnegie, Adam Grant, Steven Covey, Jay Shetty, Dr. Irving Misner, Reid Hoffman, Brené Brown, Wayne Baker, and the many thinkers before and after them. It's why we built this system.

I also believe that this system could be a useful resource for nonprofits in asking for donations, welcoming new members, and posting events. I am on the board of several nonprofit organizations, and I know they all have mountains and rocks to climb, and it isn't easy. So many of these organizations are already Needworking, and it's exciting to see. In time we will figure out a fun, unique way to involve these organizations and provide them with a value that is a twist on social media.

Nonprofits have so many great events, and they get lost in the compounding noise of social media and emails. We recently launched our Event feature for event organizers to help connect their participants. The idea is that prior to the event, an attendee can see who is attending the event in advance (and also see this after the event) and will also be able to see the Need of that person. The goal of this easier way to connect is to allow attendees a communication tool so they don't have to go to LinkedIn. Our platform will probably not scale to that of a LinkedIn or Eventbrite, and I'm okay with that.

Needworking is the perfect way for specialized requests to occur, especially for nonprofits. Earlier in the book, I mentioned Saint Vincent's Villa Maria, where I was adopted. On one of my visits as an adult, they showed me the salon that was on campus. The children on campus now are aged six to teenagers, and taking them off campus for haircuts is not feasible. The chief administrator had asked if I knew anyone that would volunteer to do on-site spa appointments for the kids. These kids come from tough home circumstances and have never been pampered. I reached out to a friend, Maria Butta, who owns Tranquille Hair and Body, and to Kelly Vo, who owned Bliss Nails. They both have come out and volunteered their time for hair and nail treatments for the kids who were interested. Those little things change lives and lift spirits, and thanks to my connections, we made that happen.

We have built Needworking for special requests just like that. Yes, it's volunteering, but not everyone is trained to cut hair and trim nails. Our system can layer requests and prioritize topics and locations.

We have built a structured system that includes Eventbrite and LinkedIn. As we discussed in previous chapters, there are tools for every type of Need out there, and we felt there could be something a little different compared to the event apps you see at conferences that then disappear until the next year. This tool could be for planners that have thousands of people attending, but it's really meant for groups of 25-150. We feel that intimate groups are really the sweet spot for what we believe is a deeper connection for networking. There are other companies that specialize in 1x event apps, and that's not our focus. We want to allow engagement after an event is finished and not rely on the reciprocity happening on another platform.

We set up a way to help event organizers and attendees in advance of an event. We have built Needworking for organizers to allow attendees to post their Needs in advance. The advantage of this is threefold:

➡ You can see who's attending and have conversations prior to the event and schedule time with them while they are there.

➡ You have a general idea of people who you feel are the best fit for you and what you are trying to accomplish.

➡ We have built in a connection piece to add people into your Ally circle. Instead of spending time connecting with them on LinkedIn, you can be connecting with others at the event.

Our goal in building out these tools and features for people is to do exactly what that gentleman in the hallway of SXSW said. It's "Efficient Networking!" Oh, I really wish he had signed on and connected with me so I could thank him personally. Mr. Whoever You Are, if you ever pick up this book, please let us know it was you.

The Need I would ask of you is to sign up for Needworking and try it out. We are building and improving the platform, so your usage and feedback is important to us. If you like it or any of the advice I've provided, we would greatly appreciate it if you upgrade your account to have a paid membership. We will have additional features for subscribers and fun collectible Maslow Badges as we explore how to grow what we have already built into a more user-friendly interface.

You can find more information and Needworking instructional videos at https://support.needworking.com. Here we provide links to Insights we have written that include snippets of the book, along with Needworking how-tos.

We have also put together a Shopify site that includes many of the books I have referenced, as well as some fun merch that you might want to own. You can help support the Needworking platform by buying a product from our store: https://needworking.myshopify.com/.

Finally, I like to ask this question:

How many times have you used the word Need in the last twenty-four hours? A Need is natural, and you shouldn't feel guilty or shunned as Needy just because you asked for help. Needworking is natural, and I used the word Need in this book approximately 560 times. It's give or take about 1% of the total makeup of everything I had to give. We sometimes don't realize how much we do in a day for others, and it's perfectly justifiable to have Needs, and asking is nothing to be ashamed of.

Embrace the power of Needs, for they are the threads that weave us together as humans. There is no shame in seeking support or lending a helping hand, for in this interconnected world, we find strength through unity. Let us embark on our collective journey of Needworking, where compassion and empathy become the guiding lights that shape a brighter tomorrow.

ACKNOWLEDGEMENTS

I also would like to thank my Needworking partners Ali Muslim and Eliot Pearson, who did an incredible job bringing Needworking to life and guiding me through the process. Ali's team was an integral part of building what was in my head and mapping out this robust platform. Thank you, Fatima and Hassan. Ali and I started the process after my father had passed away, and during the next year of development, I lost my mom and he lost his as well. We became brothers across the sea and worked in tandem to build something we hoped others could benefit from. I've known him for almost twenty years, and this was a project that really connected us, and in sha'Allah connects and helps thousands of other communities to connect and fulfill Needs.

To Kelly, who dealt with all my sleepless nights of creativity and Needworking strategizing, you've been there to hand out shirts and encourage sign-ups in whatever city we traveled to. You had my back for the toughest mountain climb I've ever had, and I love and appreciate you for your support and the hand and spirit to lift me up.

To my son DJ, who was the creativity behind the Maslow Badges and a brilliant creative mind. I can't wait to see what you build and craft next on your journey. To Devon, DJ, and Sawyer, you always inspire me to continue learning and growing on my own journey. No matter what happens.

A huge thank you to all the advertising customers who entrusted me with their business year after year, especially Randy Brooks of Edward Arthur Jewelers and Alan Davis of Princeton Sports and all of our current customers.

Jonathan Balog of Goodwill Industries of the Chesapeake, T.J. and Anita Brightman from a Bright Idea, John Coulson of Pressbox, and all of our current and past customers. I can't name all of the hundreds of clients we have served and connections that have helped us grow, but without your support we wouldn't have been in business for over a decade.

To my staff at Enradius, I'm sorry I shifted gear over to Need-working in 2021 and 2022. I felt this was something I Needed to build, and I realize it took us off course for a bit. KB, Jim, Rob, Pamela, Kevin, Lindsay, Karen, and Eliot, you were the glue that kept it all together. Thank you! I'm back!

A very special thank you to Rick Leimbach from Startup Portal (startupportal.com), who graciously spent hours upon hours teaching me about crowd and equity funding and was able to help me launch my first equity fundraise for Needworking.

Thank you to Sal Cuffari, whose innovative graphic design elevated the visual essence of this book.

To Kate Victory Hannisian, whose thoughtful editing, unwavering patience, and her expert guidance made the journey to completion smoother.

Thanks to George Stevens and Eland Mann from G Sharp Design, LLC for their extraordinary talent in crafting an awe-inspiring cover design and layout, and making this book a reality; and to Lucy Morton from LKM Editorial for proofreading the final product.

Marney Lumpkin and Amanda Garion Strategic Management & Logistics for their creative and well thought out social media posts.

To all of the Needworkers who started this journey with me from the beginning to help spread the word, thank you for continuously coming back and sharing and helping others. This book and vision wouldn't have been possible without you and your support.

We are only Needworking in the United States at this point. Canada is the next Big Rock.

Rachel Millman at Reel Media (https://reelmediavideos.com), you did an incredible job with our Needworking Tour video. It already has 30,000 views on YouTube and is growing.

THANK YOU NEEDWORKING SUPPORTERS

I wanted to take a moment to express my heartfelt gratitude for your incredible support of my Needworking.com process and platform. Your role, whether as an investor or a dedicated paid member, has been pivotal in not only launching the platform but also nurturing the entire process.

Your belief in this project has been a driving force, and I'm genuinely thankful for your contribution to its success. Your support has not only helped us grow, but has also played a key role in establishing Needworking.com as a thriving community.

Knowing that my work has found support among individuals like you is truly inspiring. It's a privilege to have your backing, and I'm excited about the journey ahead with supporters who share a vision for meaningful collaboration.

Thank you once again for being an essential part of this exciting venture. Your support has made a lasting impact, and I am truly appreciative.

John Vogel
Kelly Marcus
Nettie A Owens

Bridgette Pearce

Joe Mattiko

Roderick Herron

Joseph Zuccaro

Orsolya Herbein

Ray and Lorraine Smoot

Kyle Leslie

Rachel Heermann

David Carberry Jr.

Joseph Hlatky

Joanna Scungio

Dan Taylor

Somayeh Shojaei

Phil Larson

Alan Raisman

John Coulson

Michael Carberry

Heidi Hiller

Weygan Totanes

Sean Brooks

Margiben Varia

ORGANIZATIONS

T he following organizations offer networking opportunities and resources for businesses and professionals within their respective geographic areas. They often host events, conferences, and forums for networking and industry-specific discussions. Be sure to visit their websites for more information on membership and upcoming events.

National Associations or Networking Groups

American Society of Association Executives (ASAE)
https://www.asaecenter.org/

American Marketing Association (AMA)
https://www.ama.org/

Association for Corporate Growth (ACG)
https://www.acg.org/

Business Network International (BNI)
https://www.bni.com/

Chamber of Commerce
https://www.uschamber.com/

Entrepreneurs' Organization (EO)
https://www.eonetwork.org/

National Association of Women Business Owners (NAWBO)
https://www.nawbo.org/

National Association of Asian American Professionals (NAAAP)
https://www.naaap.org/

National Association of Hispanic Real Estate Professionals (NAHREP)
https://nahrep.org/

National Association of Professional Women (NAPW)
https://www.napw.com/

National Association of Professional Organizers (NAPO)
https://www.napo.net/

National Association of Realtors (NAR)
https://www.nar.realtor/

National Association of Broadcasters (NAB)
https://www.nab.org/

National Association of Manufacturers (NAM)
https://www.nam.org/

National Association of Professional Mortgage
Women (NAPMW)
https://www.napmw.org/

National Association of Professional Insurance Agents (PIA)
https://pianet.com/

National Association of Professional Background
Screeners (NAPBS)
https://www.napbs.com/

National Association of Professional Financial
Advisors (NAPFA)
https://www.napfa.org/

National Association of Professional Pet Sitters (NAPPS)
https://www.petsitters.org/

National Association of Professional Process Servers (NAPPS)
https://www.napps.org/

National Association of Professional Women in Construction (NAWIC)
https://www.nawic.org/

National Association of Professional Geriatric Care
Managers (NAPGCM)
https://www.caremanager.org/

National Black MBA Association (NBMBAA)
https://www.nbmbaa.org/

National Sales Network (NSN)
https://www.salesnetwork.org/

Rotary International
https://www.rotary.org/

Toastmasters International
https://www.toastmasters.org/

Young Professionals Network (YPN)
https://www.ypn.org/

Women's Business Enterprise National Council (WBENC)
https://www.wbenc.org/

Samples of Topic Related Groups/Organizations

Technology:

Technology Association of Georgia (TAG)
https://www.tagonline.org/ (Southeast)

New York Technology Council (NYTECH)
https://www.nytech.org/ (New York)

Massachusetts Technology Leadership Council (MassTLC)
https://www.masstlc.org/ (Massachusetts)

Technology Association of Oregon (TAO)
https://www.techoregon.org/ (Oregon)

Austin Technology Council (ATC)
https://www.austintechnologycouncil.org/ (Texas)

Healthcare:

Healthcare Information and Management Systems Society (HIMSS)
https://www.himss.org/ (National)

California Association of Health Plans (CAHP)
https://www.calhealthplans.org/ (California)

Florida Healthcare Association (FHA)
https://www.fhca.org/ (Florida)

Medical Group Management Association (MGMA)
https://www.mgma.com/ (National)

Ohio Hospital Association (OHA)
https://ohiohospitals.org/ (Ohio)

Regional Organizations

New England Business Association (NEBA)
https://www.newenglandbusiness.org/ (New England)

Mid-Atlantic Hispanic Chamber of Commerce (MAHCC)
https://www.mahcc.org/ (Mid-Atlantic)

Southern Economic Development Council (SEDC)
https://www.sedc.org/ (Southern states)

Midwest Technology Association (MTA)
https://www.midwesttechnologyassociation.org/ (Midwest)

Pacific Northwest Defense Coalition (PNDC)
https://www.pndc.us/ (Pacific Northwest)

Southwest Minority Supplier Development Council (SMSDC)
https://www.smsdc.org/ (Southwest)

Tri-State Black Chamber of Commerce (TSBCC)
https://www.tsbcchamber.org/ (Tri-State area)

Rocky Mountain Indian Chamber of Commerce (RMICC)
https://www.rmicc.org/ (Rocky Mountain region)

Great Lakes Women's Business Council (GLWBC)
https://www.greatlakeswbc.org/ (Great Lakes region)

Gulf Coast Energy Network (GCEN)
https://www.gulfcoastenergynetwork.org/ (Gulf Coast)

Pacesetters (Baltimore, Annapolis, Washington, DC)
https://www.baltimorepacesetters.com

Two Twelve Referral Networks
https://www.twotwelvereferrals.com/

Virginia Restaurant Lodging Travel Association
https://www.vrlta.org/

Ocean City Hotel Motel Restaurant Association (OCHMRA)
https://www.ocvisitor.com

Maryland Tourism Coalition (MTC)
https://mdtourism.org/

California Restaurant Association (CRA)
https://www.calrest.org/

RECOMMENDED RESOURCES

Books

Baker, Wayne. *All You Have to Do is Ask.* Currency, 2020.

Brown, Brené. *Daring Greatly: How the Courage to Be Vulnerable Transforms the Way We Live, Love, Parent, and Lead.* Gotham Books, 2012.

Brown, Brené. *Rising Strong: How the Ability to Reset Transforms the Way We Live, Love, Parent, and Lead.* Random House, 2015.

Buerger, Andrew. *Carrying a Flag from Pain to Passion.* Outskirts Press, 2020.

Carnegie, Dale. *How to Win Friends and Influence People.* Simon & Schuster, 1936.

Clark, Timothy. *The Four Stages of Psychological Safety: Defining the Path to Inclusion and Innovation.* Berrett-Koehler Publishers, Inc., 2020.

Clear, James. *Atomic Habits.* Random House Business Books, 2015.

Covey, Stephen. *The 7 Habits of Highly Effective People: Powerful Lessons in Personal Change.* Simon & Schuster, 1989.

Covey, Stephen. *First Things First.* Free Press, 2003.

Epler, Melinda Briana. *How to Be an Ally: Actions You Can Take for a Stronger, Happier Workplace.* McGraw Hill, 2021.

Gerber, Scott and Ryan Paugh. *Superconnector: Stop Networking and Start Building Business Relationships That Matter.* Da Capo Lifelong Books, 2018.

Grant, Adam. *Give and Take.* Penguin Books, 2014.

Harnish, Verne. *Mastering the Rockefeller Habits.* SelectBooks, 2002.

Jamal, Azim and Harvey McKinnon. *The Power of Giving: How Giving Back Enriches Us All.* TarcherPerigee, 2009.

Kaufman, Scott Barry. *Transcend: The New Science of Self-Actualization.* TarcherPerigee, 2021.

Lederman, Michelle Tillis. *The Connector's Advantage: 7 Mindsets to Grow Your Influence and Impact.* Page Two, 2019.

McKenna, Colleen. *It's Business, Not Social™: STANDOUT. Develop and Increase Your Significance over Time with Authenticity, Networking, Dedication, Open-Mindedness, Understanding, and Tenacity.* Intero Advisory, 2021.

McPherson, Susan. *The Lost Art of Connecting: The Gather, Ask, Do Method for Building Meaningful Business Relationships.* McGraw Hill, 2021.

Misner, Ivan and Brian Hilliard. *Networking Like a Pro: Turning Contacts into Connections.* Entrepreneur Press, 2009.

Parker, Priya. *The Art of Gathering: How We Meet and Why It Matters.* Penguin, 2019.

Port, Michael. *Book Yourself Solid: The Fastest, Easiest, and Most Reliable System for Getting More Clients Than You Can Handle Even if You Hate Marketing and Selling.* (Third edition). John Wiley & Sons, Inc., 2017.

Pritchett, Price. *You 2: A High Velocity Formula for Multiplying Your Personal Effectiveness in Quantum Leaps.* Pritchett LP, 2012.

Santi, Jenny. *The Giving Way to Happiness: Stories and Science Behind the Life-Changing Power of Giving.* TarcherPerigee, 2016.

Shetty, Jay. *Think Like a Monk: Train Your Mind for Peace and Purpose Every Day.* Simon & Schuster, 2020.

Sinek, Simon. *Start with Why: How Great Leaders Inspire Everyone to Take Action.* Portfolio, 2009.

Wiest, Brianna. *The Mountain Is You.* Thought Catalog Books, 2020.

Zack, Devora. *Networking for People Who Hate Networking, Second Edition: A Field Guide for Introverts, the Overwhelmed, and the Underconnected.* Berrett-Koehler Publishers, 2019.

Videos and Online Sources

Dunbar, Robin, "Why The Internet Won't Get You Any More Friends," March 12, 2014. Santa Fe Institute. https://www.youtube.com/watch?v=tRUCKxKMVTo

HubSpot, *How to Create Detailed Buyer Personas for Your Business*, 2022. https://blog.hubspot.com/marketing/buyer-persona-research

Netflix Original, *The Social Dilemma.* 2020.

Sivers, Dereck, "How To Start A Movement," TED Talk, 2010. https://www.ted.com/talks/derek_sivers_how_to_start_a_movement

Here is a more complete list at the time of this publishing of the reciprocal clubs I mentioned: https://www.centerclub.org/documents/10184/0/Reciprocal+Clubs+2023.pdf

2016 study in Nelson, S. K., Layous, K., Cole, S. W., & Lyubomirsky, S. (2016). Do unto Others or Treat Yourself? The Effects of Prosocial and Self-Focused Behavior on Psychological Flourishing.

"10 Ways To Help Others That Will Lead You To Success." John Hall, the CEO of Influence & Company. https://www.forbes.com/sites/johnhall/2013/05/26/10-ways-to-help-other s-that-will-lead-you-to-success/?sh=1d9b1ec82bce

www.ingramcontent.com/pod-product-compliance
Lightning Source LLC
LaVergne TN
LVHW051440050326
832903LV00030BD/3184